50 Chocolate Lovers' Indulgence Recipes for Home

By: Kelly Johnson

Table of Contents

- Triple Chocolate Brownies
- Chocolate Fondue with Assorted Dippers
- Dark Chocolate Mousse
- Chocolate Covered Strawberries
- Molten Lava Chocolate Cake
- White Chocolate Raspberry Cheesecake
- Nutella Stuffed Chocolate Chip Cookies
- Chocolate Dipped Pretzels
- Chocolate Banana Bread
- Chocolate Tiramisu
- Death by Chocolate Ice Cream
- Chocolate Hazelnut Truffles
- Chocolate Pecan Pie
- Chocolate Caramel Popcorn
- Chocolate Cherry Bombs
- Double Chocolate Pancakes
- Chocolate Covered Oreos
- Chocolate Peanut Butter Cups
- Chocolate Mint Ice Cream Sandwiches
- Chocolate Coconut Macaroons
- Raspberry Chocolate Tart
- Chocolate Almond Biscotti
- Chocolate Espresso Martini
- Dark Chocolate Peppermint Bark
- Chocolate Covered Caramel Apples
- Chocolate Raspberry Brownie Trifle
- Chocolate Pistachio Tart
- Mocha Chocolate Chip Cookies
- Chocolate Strawberry Shortcake
- Peanut Butter Chocolate Fudge
- Chocolate Mocha Cupcakes
- Chocolate Cherry Cheesecake Bars
- Chocolate Orange Scones
- Mexican Hot Chocolate
- Chocolate Caramel Pretzel Rods

- Triple Chocolate Waffles
- Chocolate Raspberry Crepes
- Mint Chocolate Chip Cheesecake
- Chocolate Pomegranate Clusters
- Chocolate Hazelnut Brioche
- Chocolate Covered Espresso Beans
- White Chocolate Raspberry Blondies
- Dark Chocolate Sea Salt Caramels
- Chocolate Banana Smoothie Bowl
- Chocolate Pecan Cinnamon Rolls
- Chocolate Raspberry Soufflé
- Chocolate Almond Butter Cups
- Black Forest Chocolate Cake
- Chocolate Covered Macadamia Nuts
- Chocolate Raspberry Chia Pudding

Triple Chocolate Brownies

Ingredients:

- 1 cup (2 sticks) unsalted butter
- 1 1/2 cups granulated sugar
- 1 teaspoon vanilla extract
- 4 large eggs
- 1 cup all-purpose flour
- 1/2 cup cocoa powder
- 1/4 teaspoon salt
- 1 cup semi-sweet chocolate chips
- 1/2 cup white chocolate chips
- 1/2 cup dark chocolate chips

Instructions:

Preheat your oven to 350°F (175°C). Grease a 9x13-inch baking pan and line it with parchment paper, leaving an overhang for easy removal.

In a microwave-safe bowl, melt the butter. Allow it to cool slightly.

In a large mixing bowl, combine the melted butter, sugar, and vanilla extract. Mix well.

Add the eggs one at a time, beating well after each addition.

In a separate bowl, sift together the flour, cocoa powder, and salt. Gradually add the dry ingredients to the wet ingredients, mixing until just combined.

Fold in the semi-sweet, white, and dark chocolate chips until evenly distributed in the batter.

Pour the batter into the prepared baking pan and spread it evenly.

Bake in the preheated oven for 25-30 minutes or until a toothpick inserted into the center comes out with a few moist crumbs (not wet batter).

Allow the brownies to cool completely in the pan on a wire rack.

Once cooled, use the parchment paper overhang to lift the brownies out of the pan. Cut into squares and enjoy the triple chocolate indulgence!

Chocolate Fondue with Assorted Dippers
Ingredients:

For the Chocolate Fondue:

- 1 cup dark chocolate, finely chopped
- 1/2 cup milk chocolate, finely chopped
- 1 cup heavy cream
- 2 tablespoons unsalted butter
- 1 teaspoon vanilla extract

For Assorted Dippers:

- Strawberries, washed and hulled
- Bananas, sliced
- Pineapple chunks
- Apple slices
- Pretzel rods
- Marshmallows
- Cubes of pound cake
- Rice Krispies treats, cut into bite-sized pieces
- Biscotti, broken into pieces
- Graham crackers, broken into squares

Instructions:

Prepare the Dippers:
- Wash and prepare the fruits as needed.
- Arrange all the assorted dippers on a serving platter.

Make the Chocolate Fondue:
- In a medium-sized saucepan, heat the heavy cream over medium heat until it starts to simmer but does not boil.
- Place the finely chopped dark chocolate and milk chocolate in a heatproof bowl.
- Pour the hot cream over the chopped chocolate. Let it sit for a minute to soften the chocolate.
- Stir the mixture until the chocolate is completely melted and smooth.

- Add the unsalted butter and vanilla extract, stirring until well combined.

Serve:
- Pour the melted chocolate fondue into a fondue pot or a heatproof bowl.
- Arrange the platter of assorted dippers around the fondue pot.
- Provide fondue forks or skewers for dipping.

Enjoy:
- Dip your favorite dippers into the warm chocolate fondue, coating them with the rich and creamy chocolate.
- Experiment with different combinations of dippers to create your perfect chocolate indulgence.
- Remember to be cautious with the hot chocolate, and have a delightful time enjoying the chocolate fondue with your chosen dippers!

Dark Chocolate Mousse

Ingredients:

- 8 ounces (about 225g) dark chocolate, finely chopped
- 1/4 cup (60ml) strong brewed coffee, cooled
- 3 large eggs, separated
- 1/4 cup (50g) granulated sugar
- 1 teaspoon vanilla extract
- 1 1/2 cups (360ml) heavy cream
- Optional: Dark chocolate shavings or grated chocolate for garnish

Instructions:

Melt the Dark Chocolate:
- In a heatproof bowl, melt the finely chopped dark chocolate. You can do this by placing the bowl over a pot of simmering water (double boiler) or by using short intervals in the microwave. Stir until smooth.

Add Coffee:
- Stir in the cooled brewed coffee into the melted chocolate. Mix well until combined. Set aside to cool to room temperature.

Whip Egg Whites:
- In a clean, dry bowl, whip the egg whites using an electric mixer until soft peaks form.

Beat Egg Yolks and Sugar:
- In a separate bowl, beat the egg yolks and granulated sugar until pale and slightly thickened.

Combine Chocolate and Egg Yolks:
- Gently fold the melted chocolate mixture into the egg yolk mixture until well combined.

Fold in Whipped Cream:
- In the same bowl, whip the heavy cream until soft peaks form. Fold the whipped cream into the chocolate mixture until smooth and evenly combined.

Fold in Egg Whites:
- Carefully fold the whipped egg whites into the chocolate mixture in two or three additions. Be gentle to maintain the mousse's light and airy texture.

Chill:
- Spoon the dark chocolate mousse into serving glasses or bowls. Cover and refrigerate for at least 4 hours or overnight to allow it to set.

Garnish and Serve:
- Before serving, garnish the dark chocolate mousse with dark chocolate shavings or grated chocolate, if desired.
- Serve chilled and enjoy the rich and velvety texture of this delicious dark chocolate mousse!

Chocolate Covered Strawberries

Ingredients:

- 1 pound (about 450g) fresh strawberries, washed and dried
- 8 ounces (about 225g) semisweet or dark chocolate, chopped
- 1 tablespoon coconut oil or vegetable shortening (optional, for smoother consistency)
- Optional toppings: chopped nuts, shredded coconut, sprinkles, or drizzled white chocolate

Instructions:

Prepare a Baking Sheet:
- Line a baking sheet with parchment paper or wax paper.

Melt Chocolate:
- In a heatproof bowl, melt the chopped chocolate in the microwave or over a double boiler. If using the microwave, heat in short 20-second bursts, stirring between each burst until the chocolate is completely melted.

Add Coconut Oil (Optional):
- If desired, add 1 tablespoon of coconut oil or vegetable shortening to the melted chocolate and stir until smooth. This helps achieve a smoother consistency for dipping.

Dip Strawberries:
- Hold each strawberry by the stem and dip it into the melted chocolate, allowing any excess chocolate to drip off.

Set on Baking Sheet:
- Place the chocolate-covered strawberries on the prepared baking sheet, making sure they are not touching each other.

Optional Toppings:
- While the chocolate is still wet, you can sprinkle chopped nuts, shredded coconut, or your favorite toppings on the chocolate-covered strawberries.

Allow to Set:
- Allow the chocolate-covered strawberries to set at room temperature or place them in the refrigerator for about 30 minutes to speed up the process.

Drizzle with White Chocolate (Optional):
- If desired, melt white chocolate and drizzle it over the set chocolate-covered strawberries for a decorative touch.

Serve:
- Once the chocolate is fully set, transfer the chocolate-covered strawberries to a serving platter or enjoy them directly from the baking sheet.

Enjoy:
- Serve these delightful chocolate-covered strawberries as a sweet treat for special occasions or enjoy them as a delicious and elegant dessert.

Molten Lava Chocolate Cake

Ingredients:

- 1/2 cup (1 stick) unsalted butter
- 4 ounces (about 115g) semi-sweet or bittersweet chocolate, chopped
- 1 cup powdered sugar
- 2 large eggs
- 2 egg yolks
- 1 teaspoon vanilla extract
- 1/4 cup all-purpose flour
- Pinch of salt
- Optional: Vanilla ice cream or whipped cream for serving

Instructions:

Preheat Oven:
- Preheat your oven to 425°F (220°C). Grease and flour 4 individual ramekins or custard cups.

Melt Butter and Chocolate:
- In a microwave-safe bowl or using a double boiler, melt the butter and chopped chocolate together until smooth. Stir well to combine.

Add Powdered Sugar:
- Stir in the powdered sugar into the melted chocolate mixture until well combined.

Add Eggs and Vanilla:
- Add the eggs, egg yolks, and vanilla extract to the chocolate mixture. Mix well until smooth and creamy.

Fold in Flour and Salt:
- Gently fold in the all-purpose flour and a pinch of salt until just combined. Do not overmix.

Fill Ramekins:
- Divide the batter evenly among the prepared ramekins.

Bake:
- Place the ramekins on a baking sheet and bake in the preheated oven for about 12-14 minutes or until the edges are set, but the center is still soft and gooey.

Let it Rest:

- Allow the molten lava cakes to cool for a couple of minutes before running a knife around the edges to loosen them.

Serve:
- Invert each molten lava cake onto a serving plate. The soft, gooey center should flow out, resembling molten lava.

Optional Toppings:
- Serve the molten lava chocolate cakes with a scoop of vanilla ice cream or a dollop of whipped cream if desired.

Enjoy:
- Indulge in the rich and decadent goodness of these molten lava chocolate cakes while they are warm. The contrast of the gooey center with the slightly firm edges is pure bliss for chocolate lovers.

White Chocolate Raspberry Cheesecake

Ingredients:

For the Crust:

- 1 1/2 cups graham cracker crumbs
- 1/3 cup unsalted butter, melted
- 2 tablespoons granulated sugar

For the White Chocolate Raspberry Cheesecake Filling:

- 24 ounces (about 680g) cream cheese, softened
- 1 cup granulated sugar
- 1 teaspoon vanilla extract
- 4 large eggs
- 1 cup white chocolate chips, melted and cooled
- 1/2 cup sour cream
- 1/2 cup raspberry puree (made from fresh or frozen raspberries)

For Raspberry Swirl (Optional):

- 1/2 cup raspberry puree
- 2 tablespoons granulated sugar

Instructions:

Preheat Oven:
- Preheat your oven to 325°F (160°C). Grease a 9-inch springform pan with butter or non-stick cooking spray.

Make the Crust:
- In a medium bowl, combine the graham cracker crumbs, melted butter, and 2 tablespoons of granulated sugar. Press the mixture firmly into the bottom of the prepared springform pan to form the crust.

Melt White Chocolate:
- Melt the white chocolate chips using a double boiler or in short intervals in the microwave. Allow it to cool slightly.

Prepare Raspberry Puree:

- If not using pre-made raspberry puree, blend fresh or thawed frozen raspberries in a blender until smooth. Strain to remove seeds.

Make Raspberry Swirl (Optional):
- In a small saucepan, heat 1/2 cup of raspberry puree and 2 tablespoons of granulated sugar over medium heat until it thickens slightly. Set aside to cool.

Prepare Cheesecake Filling:
- In a large bowl, beat the cream cheese until smooth. Add the granulated sugar and vanilla extract, and continue beating until well combined.
- Add the eggs one at a time, beating well after each addition.
- Mix in the melted white chocolate, sour cream, and raspberry puree until the batter is smooth and well combined.

Pour Batter Into Pan:
- Pour the cheesecake batter over the prepared crust in the springform pan.

Add Raspberry Swirl (Optional):
- If desired, drop spoonfuls of the raspberry swirl mixture onto the cheesecake batter. Use a knife or toothpick to create a marbled effect.

Bake:
- Bake in the preheated oven for about 55-65 minutes or until the center is set and the edges are lightly browned.

Cool:
- Allow the cheesecake to cool in the pan on a wire rack for at least 1 hour. Refrigerate for at least 4 hours or overnight before serving.

Serve:
- Release the springform pan, slice, and serve chilled. Enjoy the delightful combination of white chocolate and raspberry in this creamy cheesecake!

Nutella Stuffed Chocolate Chip Cookies

Ingredients:

- 1 cup (2 sticks) unsalted butter, softened
- 1 cup granulated sugar
- 1 cup brown sugar, packed
- 2 large eggs
- 1 teaspoon vanilla extract
- 3 cups all-purpose flour
- 1 teaspoon baking soda
- 1/2 teaspoon baking powder
- 1/2 teaspoon salt
- 2 cups chocolate chips
- Nutella, chilled (about 1/2 cup)

Instructions:

Preheat Oven:
- Preheat your oven to 350°F (175°C). Line baking sheets with parchment paper.

Cream Butter and Sugars:
- In a large bowl, cream together the softened butter, granulated sugar, and brown sugar until light and fluffy.

Add Eggs and Vanilla:
- Beat in the eggs one at a time, then add the vanilla extract. Mix until well combined.

Combine Dry Ingredients:
- In a separate bowl, whisk together the flour, baking soda, baking powder, and salt.

Add Dry Ingredients to Wet Ingredients:
- Gradually add the dry ingredients to the wet ingredients, mixing until just combined.

Fold in Chocolate Chips:
- Gently fold in the chocolate chips until evenly distributed throughout the cookie dough.

Chill Dough:
- For easier handling, chill the cookie dough in the refrigerator for at least 30 minutes.

Form Cookie Dough Balls:
- Scoop about 1 to 1.5 tablespoons of cookie dough and flatten it in the palm of your hand. Place a small spoonful of chilled Nutella in the center.

Seal and Roll:
- Fold the cookie dough over the Nutella, sealing the edges, and roll it into a ball. Place on the prepared baking sheets.

Bake:
- Bake in the preheated oven for 10-12 minutes or until the edges are golden but the center is still soft.

Cool:
- Allow the cookies to cool on the baking sheets for a few minutes before transferring them to a wire rack to cool completely.

Enjoy:
- Once cooled, enjoy the delicious Nutella Stuffed Chocolate Chip Cookies with a glass of milk or your favorite beverage. The gooey Nutella center adds an extra layer of indulgence to classic chocolate chip cookies.

Chocolate Dipped Pretzels

Ingredients:

- 1 cup (2 sticks) unsalted butter, softened
- 3/4 cup granulated sugar
- 3/4 cup packed brown sugar
- 2 large eggs
- 1 teaspoon vanilla extract
- 3 cups all-purpose flour
- 1 teaspoon baking soda
- 1/2 teaspoon salt
- 2 cups chocolate chips
- Nutella, chilled in the refrigerator

Instructions:

Preheat your oven to 350°F (175°C). Line baking sheets with parchment paper.
In a large bowl, cream together the softened butter, granulated sugar, and brown sugar until light and fluffy.
Add the eggs one at a time, beating well after each addition. Stir in the vanilla extract.
In a separate bowl, whisk together the flour, baking soda, and salt. Gradually add the dry ingredients to the wet ingredients, mixing until just combined.
Fold in the chocolate chips until evenly distributed throughout the cookie dough.
Scoop out portions of cookie dough and flatten each portion into a disk. Place a small spoonful of chilled Nutella in the center, then fold the edges of the cookie dough around the Nutella, sealing it completely. Shape the dough into a ball.
Place the stuffed cookie dough balls onto the prepared baking sheets, leaving space between each for spreading.
Bake in the preheated oven for 10-12 minutes or until the edges are golden but the centers are still soft.
Allow the cookies to cool on the baking sheets for a few minutes before transferring them to a wire rack to cool completely.
Enjoy the irresistible combination of chocolate chip cookies with a gooey Nutella center!

Chocolate Dipped Pretzels

Ingredients:

- Pretzel rods or pretzel twists
- 8 ounces (about 225g) dark or milk chocolate, chopped
- Assorted toppings: chopped nuts, sprinkles, shredded coconut, crushed candies (optional)

Instructions:

Line a baking sheet with parchment paper.
In a heatproof bowl, melt the chocolate using a double boiler or in short intervals in the microwave, stirring until smooth.
Dip each pretzel rod or twist into the melted chocolate, ensuring it is fully coated. Allow excess chocolate to drip off, and place the dipped pretzels on the prepared baking sheet.
While the chocolate is still wet, sprinkle your choice of toppings over the dipped pretzels.
Place the baking sheet in the refrigerator for about 15-20 minutes or until the chocolate is set.
Once set, remove the chocolate dipped pretzels from the refrigerator.
Store in an airtight container or enjoy them as a sweet and salty treat.

These Nutella Stuffed Chocolate Chip Cookies and Chocolate Dipped Pretzels make for deliciously indulgent desserts or snacks!

Chocolate Banana Bread

Ingredients:

- 3 ripe bananas, mashed
- 1/2 cup (1 stick) unsalted butter, melted
- 1 teaspoon vanilla extract
- 2 large eggs
- 1 cup granulated sugar
- 1 1/2 cups all-purpose flour
- 1/2 cup cocoa powder
- 1 teaspoon baking soda
- 1/2 teaspoon baking powder
- 1/2 teaspoon salt
- 1 cup chocolate chips (semisweet or milk chocolate)

Instructions:

Preheat your oven to 350°F (175°C). Grease a 9x5-inch loaf pan and line it with parchment paper for easy removal.

In a large mixing bowl, mash the ripe bananas with a fork.

Melt the butter in a microwave-safe bowl and let it cool slightly. Add the melted butter to the mashed bananas.

Stir in the vanilla extract and add the eggs one at a time, mixing well after each addition.

In a separate bowl, whisk together the flour, cocoa powder, baking soda, baking powder, and salt.

Gradually add the dry ingredients to the wet ingredients, stirring until just combined. Be careful not to overmix.

Fold in the chocolate chips until evenly distributed in the batter.

Pour the batter into the prepared loaf pan, spreading it evenly.

Bake in the preheated oven for approximately 60-70 minutes or until a toothpick inserted into the center comes out with a few moist crumbs (not wet batter).

Allow the chocolate banana bread to cool in the pan for about 10 minutes before transferring it to a wire rack to cool completely.

Once cooled, slice and enjoy the moist and chocolaty goodness of this delightful Chocolate Banana Bread!

Tip: Feel free to add chopped nuts, such as walnuts or pecans, for an extra crunch if desired.

Chocolate Tiramisu

Ingredients:

For the Coffee Soaking Liquid:

- 1 cup strong brewed coffee, cooled
- 2 tablespoons coffee liqueur (e.g., Kahlúa) - optional
- 1 tablespoon sugar

For the Chocolate Mascarpone Filling:

- 1 1/2 cups heavy cream
- 8 ounces (about 225g) mascarpone cheese, softened
- 1 cup powdered sugar
- 1 teaspoon vanilla extract
- 1/2 cup unsweetened cocoa powder
- 1 cup chocolate shavings or grated chocolate, for garnish

For Assembling:

- 24-30 ladyfinger cookies (savoiardi)

Instructions:

Prepare the Coffee Soaking Liquid:
- In a shallow dish, combine the cooled strong brewed coffee, coffee liqueur (if using), and sugar. Stir until the sugar is dissolved. Set aside.

Prepare the Chocolate Mascarpone Filling:
- In a large mixing bowl, whip the heavy cream until stiff peaks form.
- In another bowl, combine the mascarpone cheese, powdered sugar, vanilla extract, and unsweetened cocoa powder. Mix until smooth.
- Gently fold the whipped cream into the mascarpone mixture until well combined.

Assembling the Chocolate Tiramisu:
- Dip each ladyfinger into the coffee soaking liquid for a couple of seconds, ensuring they are soaked but not overly soggy.

- Arrange a layer of soaked ladyfingers in the bottom of a serving dish or individual glasses.
- Spread half of the chocolate mascarpone filling over the ladyfingers layer, smoothing it with a spatula.
- Repeat the process with another layer of soaked ladyfingers and the remaining chocolate mascarpone filling.

Chill:
- Cover the dish or glasses with plastic wrap and refrigerate the chocolate tiramisu for at least 4 hours or overnight to allow the flavors to meld and the dessert to set.

Garnish and Serve:
- Before serving, garnish the top with chocolate shavings or grated chocolate.
- Slice and serve the chocolate tiramisu chilled, savoring the rich and decadent layers of coffee-soaked ladyfingers and chocolate mascarpone filling.

Enjoy this delightful twist on the classic tiramisu with the added richness of chocolate!

Death by Chocolate Ice Cream

Ingredients:

For the Chocolate Ice Cream Base:

- 2 cups heavy cream
- 1 cup whole milk
- 3/4 cup granulated sugar
- 3/4 cup unsweetened cocoa powder
- 4 ounces (about 115g) dark chocolate, finely chopped
- 1 teaspoon vanilla extract
- Pinch of salt

For Chocolate Add-ins:

- 1 cup chocolate fudge sauce (store-bought or homemade)
- 1 cup brownie chunks (store-bought or homemade)
- 1/2 cup chocolate chips or chunks

Optional Toppings:

- Whipped cream
- Chocolate shavings
- Chopped nuts

Instructions:

Prepare the Chocolate Ice Cream Base:
- In a medium saucepan, whisk together the heavy cream, whole milk, granulated sugar, and unsweetened cocoa powder over medium heat. Stir until the sugar is dissolved and the mixture is well combined.
- Add the finely chopped dark chocolate to the saucepan and continue stirring until the chocolate is melted and the mixture is smooth.
- Remove the saucepan from heat, and stir in the vanilla extract and a pinch of salt. Allow the chocolate ice cream base to cool completely.

Churn the Ice Cream:

- Once the chocolate ice cream base is cooled, transfer it to an ice cream maker and churn according to the manufacturer's instructions.

Add Chocolate Add-ins:
- During the last few minutes of churning, add in the chocolate fudge sauce, brownie chunks, and chocolate chips or chunks. Let the ice cream maker incorporate them into the ice cream.

Transfer and Freeze:
- Transfer the churned ice cream with the chocolate add-ins to a lidded container.
- Swirl in additional fudge sauce or brownie chunks if desired.
- Cover the container with a lid or plastic wrap and freeze for at least 4 hours or until the ice cream is firm.

Serve:
- Scoop the Death by Chocolate Ice Cream into bowls or cones.

Optional Toppings:
- Top each serving with whipped cream, chocolate shavings, or chopped nuts for an extra indulgent experience.

Enjoy:
- Relish in the decadence of this "Death by Chocolate" ice cream, featuring a rich chocolate base and loaded with fudge, brownie chunks, and chocolate chips. It's a heavenly treat for chocolate lovers!

Chocolate Hazelnut Truffles

Ingredients:
1 cup (about 150g) hazelnuts, toasted and finely chopped
1 cup (175g) high-quality dark chocolate, chopped
1/2 cup (120ml) heavy cream
2 tablespoons unsalted butter
1 teaspoon vanilla extract
A pinch of salt
Cocoa powder, chopped nuts, or melted chocolate for coating (optional)

Instructions:

Toast Hazelnuts:

Preheat your oven to 350°F (180°C).
Spread the hazelnuts on a baking sheet and toast them in the oven for about 10-15 minutes or until the skins start to crack.
Rub the toasted hazelnuts in a kitchen towel to remove the skins. Let them cool completely.

Prepare Ganache:

In a saucepan, heat the heavy cream over medium heat until it just starts to simmer.
Place the chopped chocolate in a heatproof bowl and pour the hot cream over it. Let it sit for a minute to melt the chocolate.
Stir the mixture until smooth, and then add the butter, vanilla extract, and a pinch of salt. Mix until well combined.

Add Hazelnuts:

Fold in the finely chopped hazelnuts into the chocolate ganache. Make sure the mixture is well combined.
Allow the mixture to cool to room temperature, and then refrigerate for at least 2 hours or until it firms up.

Shape Truffles:

Once the mixture is firm, use a spoon or a melon baller to scoop out small portions and roll them into round truffle balls.
If the mixture is too sticky, you can dust your hands with cocoa powder to make the rolling process easier.

Coat Truffles (Optional):

Roll the truffles in cocoa powder, finely chopped nuts, or dip them in melted chocolate for an extra layer of indulgence.
Chill:

Place the shaped truffles on a parchment-lined tray and refrigerate for another 30 minutes to set.
Serve:

Once the truffles are fully set, transfer them to an airtight container and store in the refrigerator until ready to serve.
Enjoy these delicious Chocolate Hazelnut Truffles as a sweet treat or consider gifting them to friends and family!

Chocolate Pecan Pie

Ingredients:

For the Pie Crust:

- 1 1/4 cups all-purpose flour
- 1/2 cup unsalted butter, cold and cut into small cubes
- 1/4 cup granulated sugar
- 1/4 teaspoon salt
- 2-3 tablespoons ice water

For the Filling:

- 1 cup pecan halves
- 1 cup semisweet or bittersweet chocolate chips
- 3 large eggs
- 1 cup light corn syrup
- 1/2 cup granulated sugar
- 1/4 cup brown sugar, packed
- 1/4 cup unsalted butter, melted
- 1 teaspoon vanilla extract
- 1/4 teaspoon salt

Instructions:

1. Prepare the Pie Crust:

- In a food processor, combine the flour, sugar, and salt. Pulse to mix.
- Add the cold butter and pulse until the mixture resembles coarse crumbs.
- Gradually add ice water, one tablespoon at a time, and pulse until the dough comes together.
- Form the dough into a disk, wrap it in plastic wrap, and refrigerate for at least 1 hour.

2. Roll Out the Pie Crust:

- Preheat your oven to 350°F (175°C).

- On a floured surface, roll out the chilled dough into a 9-inch pie crust. Place it in a pie dish and trim the edges. Crimp the edges or decorate as desired.

3. Prepare the Filling:

- In a bowl, whisk together the eggs, corn syrup, granulated sugar, brown sugar, melted butter, vanilla extract, and salt until well combined.
- Stir in the pecan halves and chocolate chips until evenly distributed.

4. Assemble the Pie:

- Pour the pecan and chocolate filling into the prepared pie crust.

5. Bake:

- Place the pie in the preheated oven and bake for 50-60 minutes or until the center is set. The pie should have a slight jiggle but not be liquid in the center.
- If the crust edges start to brown too quickly, you can cover them with aluminum foil.

6. Cool and Serve:

- Allow the chocolate pecan pie to cool completely before slicing.
- Serve slices on their own or with a dollop of whipped cream or a scoop of vanilla ice cream.

Enjoy the decadent and flavorful Chocolate Pecan Pie!

Chocolate Caramel Popcorn

Ingredients:

- 12 cups popped popcorn (about 1/2 cup unpopped kernels)
- 1 cup (2 sticks) unsalted butter
- 1 cup light brown sugar, packed
- 1/2 cup light corn syrup
- 1/2 teaspoon salt
- 1/4 teaspoon baking soda
- 1 teaspoon vanilla extract
- 1 to 2 cups chocolate chips or chocolate chunks (milk or dark chocolate, according to your preference)

Instructions:

1. Preheat and Prepare:

- Preheat your oven to 250°F (120°C). Line two large baking sheets with parchment paper or silicone baking mats.

2. Pop the Popcorn:

- Pop the popcorn and place it in a large mixing bowl. Make sure to remove any unpopped kernels.

3. Prepare Caramel Sauce:

- In a saucepan over medium heat, melt the butter. Stir in the brown sugar, corn syrup, and salt.
- Bring the mixture to a boil, stirring continuously. Once it reaches a boil, let it cook for 4-5 minutes without stirring.

4. Add Baking Soda and Vanilla:

- Remove the caramel sauce from heat and stir in the baking soda and vanilla extract. The mixture will bubble up.

5. Coat Popcorn:

- Quickly pour the caramel sauce over the popped popcorn. Use a rubber spatula to gently fold and coat the popcorn evenly.

6. Bake:

- Spread the coated popcorn onto the prepared baking sheets in an even layer.
- Bake in the preheated oven for 45-60 minutes, stirring every 15 minutes to ensure even coating.

7. Cool:

- Allow the caramel popcorn to cool completely on the baking sheets. It will continue to crisp up as it cools.

8. Melt Chocolate:

- Melt the chocolate chips or chunks using a microwave or a double boiler. Stir until smooth.

9. Drizzle Chocolate:

- Drizzle the melted chocolate over the cooled caramel popcorn. You can use a spoon, fork, or even transfer the melted chocolate to a piping bag for a more controlled drizzle.

10. Let it Set:

- Allow the chocolate to set before breaking the popcorn into clusters.

11. Serve and Enjoy:

- Once the chocolate has set, transfer the Chocolate Caramel Popcorn to a serving bowl or individual bags.

This Chocolate Caramel Popcorn is perfect for movie nights, parties, or as a sweet snack anytime!

Chocolate Cherry Bombs

Ingredients:

- Maraschino cherries, drained and patted dry
- 1 cup chocolate chips (dark, milk, or semi-sweet)
- 1 tablespoon coconut oil or vegetable shortening
- Optional: White chocolate for drizzling
- Optional: Sprinkles or chopped nuts for decoration

Instructions:

1. Prepare Cherries:

- Drain the maraschino cherries and pat them dry with paper towels. It's essential to remove excess moisture to help the chocolate adhere better.

2. Melt Chocolate:

- In a microwave-safe bowl or using a double boiler, melt the chocolate chips with coconut oil or vegetable shortening. Stir until smooth.

3. Coat Cherries:

- Dip each dried cherry into the melted chocolate, ensuring it is well coated. You can use a fork or toothpick to help with the dipping process.
- Allow any excess chocolate to drip off before placing the chocolate-covered cherry on a parchment paper-lined tray.

4. Set:

- Allow the chocolate-covered cherries to set in the refrigerator for about 15-20 minutes or until the chocolate hardens.

5. Optional Drizzle:

- If desired, melt white chocolate in the same way as the dark chocolate and drizzle it over the set chocolate-covered cherries for a decorative touch.

6. Decorate:

   - While the chocolate is still wet, you can sprinkle chopped nuts or colorful sprinkles on top for added texture and flavor.

7. Chill:

   - Place the tray back in the refrigerator for an additional 10-15 minutes to let any additional layers of chocolate or decorations set.

8. Serve:

   - Once the chocolate is completely set, you can transfer the Chocolate Cherry Bombs to a serving plate or store them in an airtight container in the refrigerator until ready to serve.

These Chocolate Cherry Bombs make for a delightful and sweet treat, perfect for special occasions, dessert tables, or as a homemade gift for friends and family. Enjoy!

Double Chocolate Pancakes

Ingredients:

- 1 cup all-purpose flour
- 1/4 cup unsweetened cocoa powder
- 1/4 cup granulated sugar
- 1 tablespoon baking powder
- 1/4 teaspoon salt
- 1 cup milk
- 1 large egg
- 2 tablespoons unsalted butter, melted
- 1 teaspoon vanilla extract
- 1/2 cup chocolate chips (semisweet or dark)

Instructions:

1. Mix Dry Ingredients:

- In a large mixing bowl, whisk together the flour, cocoa powder, sugar, baking powder, and salt.

2. Combine Wet Ingredients:

- In another bowl, whisk together the milk, egg, melted butter, and vanilla extract.

3. Combine Wet and Dry Ingredients:

- Pour the wet ingredients into the dry ingredients and stir until just combined. Be careful not to overmix; it's okay if there are a few lumps.

4. Add Chocolate Chips:

- Gently fold in the chocolate chips into the batter.

5. Heat the Griddle or Pan:

- Preheat a griddle or a non-stick frying pan over medium heat. Lightly grease it with butter or cooking spray.

6. Cook Pancakes:

- Pour 1/4 cup of batter onto the hot griddle for each pancake. Cook until bubbles form on the surface, then flip and cook the other side until it's cooked through.

7. Keep Warm:

- Keep the cooked pancakes warm by placing them on a plate in a low-temperature oven while you cook the remaining batter.

8. Serve:

- Serve the double chocolate pancakes warm, either plain or with your favorite toppings such as whipped cream, maple syrup, or additional chocolate chips.

9. Optional Garnish:

- If you want to add an extra chocolatey touch, drizzle some melted chocolate over the pancakes before serving.

These Double Chocolate Pancakes are a delightful treat for breakfast or brunch, and they're sure to satisfy any chocolate lover's cravings!

Chocolate Covered Oreos

Ingredients:

- Oreos (as many as you'd like to make)
- 8 to 12 ounces of high-quality chocolate (dark, milk, or white chocolate)
- Optional: Sprinkles, crushed nuts, or other toppings for decoration

Instructions:

1. Prepare a Baking Sheet:

- Line a baking sheet with parchment paper or a silicone baking mat. This will prevent the chocolate-covered Oreos from sticking.

2. Melt the Chocolate:

- Break the chocolate into small, uniform pieces for easy melting.
- Melt the chocolate using a double boiler or in the microwave. If using the microwave, heat in 20-30 second intervals, stirring between each interval until the chocolate is completely melted and smooth.

3. Dip Oreos in Chocolate:

- Using a fork or dipping tool, gently lower each Oreo into the melted chocolate, ensuring that it is fully coated. Allow excess chocolate to drip off.

4. Place on Baking Sheet:

- Place the chocolate-covered Oreos on the prepared baking sheet, leaving space between each one.

5. Optional Toppings:

- If desired, sprinkle the chocolate-covered Oreos with toppings like colorful sprinkles, crushed nuts, or edible glitter before the chocolate sets.

6. Set the Chocolate:

- Allow the chocolate-covered Oreos to set. You can speed up the process by placing them in the refrigerator for about 15-20 minutes.

7. Store or Serve:

- Once the chocolate has fully set, you can store the Chocolate Covered Oreos in an airtight container at room temperature. Alternatively, wrap them individually in cellophane or place them in decorative bags for gifting.

8. Enjoy:

- Serve these delicious treats as a delightful snack or dessert. They're great for parties, celebrations, or as a sweet gift for friends and family.

These Chocolate Covered Oreos are versatile and can be customized for various occasions. Get creative with different types of chocolate, toppings, and even food coloring for a festive touch.

Chocolate Peanut Butter Cups

Ingredients:

- 1 cup chocolate chips (dark, milk, or semi-sweet)
- 1 tablespoon coconut oil or vegetable shortening
- 1/2 cup creamy peanut butter
- 2 tablespoons powdered sugar
- 1/2 teaspoon vanilla extract
- A pinch of salt (if using unsalted peanut butter)

Instructions:

1. Prepare Muffin Tin:

- Line a muffin tin with paper cupcake liners.

2. Melt Chocolate:

- In a microwave-safe bowl or using a double boiler, melt the chocolate chips with coconut oil or vegetable shortening. Stir until smooth.

3. Coat Bottom of Liners:

- Spoon a small amount of melted chocolate into the bottom of each cupcake liner, spreading it to coat the bottom and slightly up the sides. Reserve some chocolate for the tops.

4. Set Chocolate:

- Place the muffin tin in the refrigerator or freezer for a few minutes to set the bottom layer of chocolate.

5. Prepare Peanut Butter Filling:

- In a separate bowl, mix together the peanut butter, powdered sugar, vanilla extract, and salt (if using). Adjust the sweetness and consistency according to your preference.

6. Add Peanut Butter Layer:

   - Spoon a small amount of the peanut butter mixture over the set chocolate layer in each cup.

7. Top with Chocolate:

   - Pour the remaining melted chocolate over the peanut butter layer, covering it completely.

8. Set and Chill:

   - Return the muffin tin to the refrigerator or freezer and let the Chocolate Peanut Butter Cups set completely. This will take approximately 30 minutes.

9. Serve:

   - Once set, peel off the paper liners and serve the Chocolate Peanut Butter Cups. Store any leftovers in an airtight container in the refrigerator.

These homemade Chocolate Peanut Butter Cups are a delightful treat that you can customize to suit your taste preferences. Experiment with different types of chocolate, add-ins, or even try using crunchy peanut butter for extra texture. Enjoy!

Chocolate Mint Ice Cream Sandwiches

Ingredients:

For the Chocolate Cookies:

- 1 cup all-purpose flour
- 1/2 cup unsweetened cocoa powder
- 1/2 teaspoon baking soda
- 1/4 teaspoon salt
- 1/2 cup unsalted butter, softened
- 1/2 cup granulated sugar
- 1/2 cup brown sugar, packed
- 1 large egg
- 1 teaspoon vanilla extract

For the Mint Ice Cream:

- 2 cups mint chocolate chip ice cream (or your favorite mint-flavored ice cream)

Instructions:

1. Prepare Chocolate Cookies:

- Preheat your oven to 350°F (175°C). Line a baking sheet with parchment paper.
- In a bowl, whisk together the flour, cocoa powder, baking soda, and salt. Set aside.
- In another bowl, using an electric mixer, cream together the softened butter, granulated sugar, and brown sugar until light and fluffy.
- Add the egg and vanilla extract to the butter-sugar mixture and beat until well combined.
- Gradually add the dry ingredients to the wet ingredients, mixing until just combined.
- Drop rounded tablespoons of cookie dough onto the prepared baking sheet, spacing them about 2 inches apart.
- Bake in the preheated oven for 10-12 minutes or until the edges are set. Allow the cookies to cool completely.

2. Assemble Ice Cream Sandwiches:

- Once the cookies are completely cooled, remove the mint chocolate chip ice cream from the freezer and let it soften slightly.
- Place a scoop of ice cream onto the flat side of one cookie. Top it with another cookie, pressing down gently to create a sandwich.
- Repeat the process with the remaining cookies and ice cream.

3. Freeze:

- Place the assembled ice cream sandwiches in the freezer for at least 1-2 hours or until the ice cream is firm.

4. Serve:

- Once the ice cream is fully frozen, the Chocolate Mint Ice Cream Sandwiches are ready to be enjoyed. Serve them immediately and savor the delightful combination of chocolate and mint.

5. Optional: Decorate:

- Roll the edges of the ice cream sandwiches in chopped nuts, sprinkles, or mini chocolate chips for a decorative touch.

These Chocolate Mint Ice Cream Sandwiches are a perfect treat for warm days or any time you're craving a refreshing and sweet combination. Enjoy!

Chocolate Coconut Macaroons

Ingredients:

- 3 cups shredded coconut (sweetened)
- 3/4 cup sweetened condensed milk
- 1 teaspoon vanilla extract
- 2 large egg whites
- 1/4 teaspoon salt
- 1 cup semi-sweet or dark chocolate chips
- 1 tablespoon coconut oil (optional, for smoother chocolate coating)

Instructions:

1. Preheat Oven:

- Preheat your oven to 325°F (163°C). Line a baking sheet with parchment paper.

2. Mix Ingredients:

- In a large mixing bowl, combine the shredded coconut, sweetened condensed milk, and vanilla extract. Mix well until all the coconut is evenly coated.
- In a separate bowl, whip the egg whites with salt until stiff peaks form.
- Gently fold the whipped egg whites into the coconut mixture until well combined. Be careful not to deflate the egg whites too much.

3. Form Macaroons:

- Drop rounded tablespoons of the coconut mixture onto the prepared baking sheet, spacing them about 1-2 inches apart.

4. Bake:

- Bake in the preheated oven for 15-18 minutes or until the edges are golden brown. Keep an eye on them to prevent burning.

5. Cool:

- Allow the macaroons to cool on the baking sheet for a few minutes before transferring them to a wire rack to cool completely.

6. Chocolate Coating:

- In a microwave-safe bowl or using a double boiler, melt the chocolate chips (and coconut oil if using) until smooth.

7. Dip and Coat:

- Dip the bottom of each cooled macaroon into the melted chocolate, allowing any excess to drip off.
- Place the chocolate-coated macaroons on a parchment-lined tray or wire rack to set.

8. Set Chocolate:

- Allow the chocolate to set at room temperature or speed up the process by placing the macaroons in the refrigerator for about 15-20 minutes.

9. Serve:

- Once the chocolate is fully set, your Chocolate Coconut Macaroons are ready to be served. Store any leftovers in an airtight container at room temperature.

Enjoy these delicious Chocolate Coconut Macaroons as a sweet treat or share them with friends and family. They're perfect for any occasion!

Raspberry Chocolate Tart

Ingredients:

For the Chocolate Tart Shell:

- 1 1/4 cups all-purpose flour
- 1/3 cup cocoa powder
- 1/2 cup unsalted butter, cold and cut into small pieces
- 1/4 cup granulated sugar
- 1/4 teaspoon salt
- 1 large egg yolk
- 2 tablespoons ice water

For the Chocolate Ganache:

- 1 cup dark chocolate chips or chopped dark chocolate
- 1/2 cup heavy cream

For the Raspberry Topping:

- 2 cups fresh raspberries, washed and patted dry
- 2 tablespoons seedless raspberry jam, melted

Optional Garnish:

- Powdered sugar for dusting
- Fresh mint leaves

Instructions:

1. Prepare the Chocolate Tart Shell:

- In a food processor, combine the flour, cocoa powder, cold butter, sugar, and salt. Pulse until the mixture resembles coarse crumbs.
- In a small bowl, whisk together the egg yolk and ice water. Add this mixture to the food processor and pulse until the dough comes together.

- Turn the dough out onto a floured surface and shape it into a disk. Wrap it in plastic wrap and refrigerate for at least 30 minutes.
- Preheat your oven to 375°F (190°C).
- Roll out the chilled dough on a floured surface and line a tart pan with it. Trim any excess dough.
- Prick the bottom of the crust with a fork, line it with parchment paper, and fill it with pie weights or dried beans.
- Bake the tart shell for about 15 minutes. Remove the parchment and weights and bake for an additional 5-10 minutes or until the crust is cooked through. Let it cool completely.

2. Make the Chocolate Ganache:

- Place the dark chocolate in a heatproof bowl.
- In a saucepan, heat the heavy cream until it just starts to simmer. Pour the hot cream over the chocolate. Let it sit for a minute, then stir until smooth and glossy.
- Pour the chocolate ganache into the cooled tart shell. Spread it evenly using a spatula. Allow it to set for at least 30 minutes or until firm.

3. Arrange Raspberries:

- Once the chocolate ganache has set, arrange the fresh raspberries on top.
- Brush the melted raspberry jam over the raspberries to give them a shiny glaze.

4. Optional Garnish:

- Dust the tart with powdered sugar and garnish with fresh mint leaves for an extra touch of elegance.

5. Chill and Serve:

- Refrigerate the tart for at least 2 hours before serving to allow the ganache to fully set.
- Slice and serve the Raspberry Chocolate Tart chilled. Enjoy the combination of rich chocolate, fresh raspberries, and buttery crust!

This tart makes a stunning dessert for special occasions or a delightful treat for any chocolate and raspberry lover.

Chocolate Almond Biscotti

Ingredients:

- 2 cups all-purpose flour
- 1/2 cup unsweetened cocoa powder
- 1 teaspoon baking powder
- 1/4 teaspoon salt
- 1/2 cup unsalted butter, softened
- 1 cup granulated sugar
- 2 large eggs
- 1 teaspoon vanilla extract
- 1 cup chopped almonds, toasted
- 1 cup semisweet or dark chocolate chips

Instructions:

1. Preheat Oven:

- Preheat your oven to 350°F (175°C). Line a baking sheet with parchment paper.

2. Toast Almonds:

- Spread the chopped almonds on a baking sheet and toast them in the preheated oven for about 8-10 minutes or until they become fragrant. Allow them to cool.

3. Mix Dry Ingredients:

- In a bowl, whisk together the flour, cocoa powder, baking powder, and salt. Set aside.

4. Cream Butter and Sugar:

- In a separate bowl, cream together the softened butter and granulated sugar until light and fluffy.

5. Add Eggs and Vanilla:

- Add the eggs one at a time, beating well after each addition. Mix in the vanilla extract.

6. Combine Wet and Dry Ingredients:

- Gradually add the dry ingredients to the wet ingredients, mixing until just combined.

7. Add Almonds and Chocolate Chips:

- Fold in the toasted chopped almonds and chocolate chips until evenly distributed in the dough.

8. Form Biscotti Logs:

- Divide the dough in half. On a floured surface, shape each portion into a log about 12 inches long and 2 inches wide. Place them on the prepared baking sheet, leaving space between them.

9. Bake:

- Bake the logs in the preheated oven for 25-30 minutes or until firm to the touch.

10. Cool and Slice:

- Allow the biscotti logs to cool on the baking sheet for about 15 minutes. Reduce the oven temperature to 325°F (163°C).
- Using a sharp knife, slice the logs into biscotti about 1/2 to 3/4 inch thick.

11. Second Bake:

- Arrange the biscotti cut side down on the baking sheet. Bake for an additional 15-20 minutes or until the biscotti are dry and crisp.

12. Cool Completely:

- Allow the Chocolate Almond Biscotti to cool completely on a wire rack.

13. Optional: Dip in Chocolate (Optional):

- Melt additional chocolate (if desired) and dip one end of each biscotti into the melted chocolate. Allow them to set before serving.

Enjoy your homemade Chocolate Almond Biscotti with a cup of coffee or tea! Store them in an airtight container for longer shelf life.

Chocolate Espresso Martini

Ingredients:

- 1 oz (30 ml) vodka
- 1 oz (30 ml) coffee liqueur (e.g., Kahlúa)
- 1 oz (30 ml) chocolate liqueur (e.g., Godiva)
- 1 oz (30 ml) freshly brewed espresso, cooled
- Ice cubes
- Chocolate shavings or coffee beans for garnish (optional)

Instructions:

1. Brew Espresso:

- Brew a shot of espresso and let it cool to room temperature.

2. Prepare Glass:

- Chill a martini glass in the freezer or by filling it with ice water.

3. Combine Ingredients:

- In a shaker filled with ice, combine the vodka, coffee liqueur, chocolate liqueur, and the cooled espresso.

4. Shake:

- Shake the mixture well for about 10-15 seconds to chill the ingredients and create a frothy texture.

5. Strain:

- Remove the ice from the chilled martini glass and strain the cocktail into the glass.

6. Garnish (Optional):

- Garnish the Chocolate Espresso Martini with chocolate shavings or coffee beans for an extra touch of elegance.

7. Serve:

- Serve the Chocolate Espresso Martini immediately while it's cold.

This cocktail is perfect for those who enjoy the combination of chocolate and coffee with a hint of vodka. It's a great after-dinner drink or a sophisticated treat for a special occasion. Enjoy responsibly!

Dark Chocolate Peppermint Bark

Ingredients:

- 12 ounces dark chocolate (70% cocoa or your preferred dark chocolate)
- 1 cup white chocolate chips or chunks
- 1/2 teaspoon peppermint extract
- Crushed peppermint candies or candy canes for topping

Instructions:

1. Prepare Baking Sheet:

   - Line a baking sheet with parchment paper or a silicone baking mat. Set aside.

2. Melt Dark Chocolate:

   - Chop the dark chocolate into small, uniform pieces for easy melting.
   - In a heatproof bowl, melt the dark chocolate using a double boiler or in the microwave. If using the microwave, heat in 20-30 second intervals, stirring between each interval until the chocolate is completely melted and smooth.

3. Add Peppermint Extract:

   - Once the dark chocolate is melted, stir in the peppermint extract until well combined.

4. Spread Dark Chocolate:

   - Pour the melted dark chocolate onto the prepared baking sheet. Use a spatula to spread it into an even layer.

5. Melt White Chocolate:

   - In a separate bowl, melt the white chocolate using the same method as the dark chocolate.

6. Add White Chocolate:

- Drizzle the melted white chocolate over the dark chocolate layer. Use a toothpick or a skewer to create swirls or patterns.

7. Create Marbled Effect:

- Use a knife or spatula to create a marbled effect by gently swirling the two chocolates together.

8. Add Peppermint Topping:

- Sprinkle the crushed peppermint candies or candy cane pieces over the top of the chocolate while it's still melted.

9. Set and Chill:

- Place the baking sheet in the refrigerator for at least 1-2 hours or until the chocolate is fully set.

10. Break Into Pieces:

- Once the Dark Chocolate Peppermint Bark is completely set, use your hands or a knife to break it into bite-sized pieces.

11. Serve or Gift:

- Serve the peppermint bark on a festive plate or package it in decorative bags or boxes for a delightful holiday gift.

This Dark Chocolate Peppermint Bark is not only delicious but also makes for a beautiful and festive treat during the holiday season. Enjoy the combination of rich dark chocolate and the cool, refreshing taste of peppermint!

Chocolate Covered Caramel Apples

Ingredients:

- 6 medium-sized apples (Granny Smith or your preferred variety)
- 1 (14-ounce) bag of soft caramels, unwrapped
- 2 tablespoons water
- 8 ounces high-quality chocolate (dark, milk, or white), chopped
- Assorted toppings (chopped nuts, sprinkles, crushed cookies, etc.)
- Wooden or plastic apple sticks

Instructions:

1. Prepare Apples:

- Wash and thoroughly dry the apples. Remove the stems and insert wooden or plastic sticks into the tops of the apples where the stems were.

2. Melt Caramels:

- In a medium-sized saucepan, combine the unwrapped caramels and water. Heat over medium-low heat, stirring constantly until the caramels are fully melted and smooth.

3. Coat Apples in Caramel:

- Dip each apple into the melted caramel, turning and coating it evenly. Allow any excess caramel to drip off, and place the caramel-coated apples on a parchment-lined tray.

4. Set Caramel:

- Allow the caramel to set for a few minutes. You can speed up the process by placing the apples in the refrigerator for about 15-20 minutes.

5. Melt Chocolate:

- In a heatproof bowl, melt the chocolate using a double boiler or in the microwave. If using the microwave, heat in 20-30 second intervals, stirring between each interval until the chocolate is completely melted and smooth.

6. Coat Caramel Apples in Chocolate:

- Dip each caramel-coated apple into the melted chocolate, turning and coating it evenly. Allow any excess chocolate to drip off.

7. Add Toppings:

- While the chocolate is still wet, roll the chocolate-covered apples in your preferred toppings, such as chopped nuts, sprinkles, or crushed cookies.

8. Set Chocolate:

- Place the chocolate-covered caramel apples on the parchment-lined tray and allow them to set completely. You can refrigerate them to speed up the process.

9. Serve or Gift:

- Once the chocolate is fully set, your Chocolate Covered Caramel Apples are ready to be enjoyed. Serve them at your next gathering or package them in clear bags with festive ribbons for a sweet gift.

These Chocolate Covered Caramel Apples are a fun and tasty treat that combines the classic flavors of caramel and chocolate with the freshness of apples. Enjoy the sweet and crunchy goodness!

Chocolate Raspberry Brownie Trifle

Ingredients:

For the Brownies:

- 1 batch of your favorite chocolate brownies (homemade or store-bought)

For the Raspberry Sauce:

- 2 cups fresh or frozen raspberries
- 1/4 cup granulated sugar
- 1 tablespoon lemon juice

For the Chocolate Pudding Layer:

- 2 cups chocolate pudding (homemade or store-bought)

For the Whipped Cream:

- 1 cup heavy cream
- 2 tablespoons powdered sugar
- 1 teaspoon vanilla extract

Optional Garnish:

- Fresh raspberries
- Chocolate shavings or curls

Instructions:

1. Prepare Brownies:

- Bake a batch of your favorite chocolate brownies according to the recipe instructions. Allow them to cool completely and cut them into bite-sized pieces.

2. Make Raspberry Sauce:

- In a saucepan, combine the raspberries, sugar, and lemon juice. Cook over medium heat until the raspberries break down and the mixture thickens, about 8-10 minutes. Strain the sauce to remove seeds and let it cool.

3. Prepare Chocolate Pudding:

- Prepare the chocolate pudding according to the package instructions or your favorite homemade recipe. Allow it to cool.

4. Make Whipped Cream:

- In a chilled bowl, whip the heavy cream until soft peaks form. Add the powdered sugar and vanilla extract, then continue whipping until stiff peaks form.

5. Assemble the Trifle:

- In a trifle dish or individual serving glasses, start layering the components:
    - Begin with a layer of chocolate brownie pieces.
    - Drizzle a portion of the raspberry sauce over the brownies.
    - Add a layer of chocolate pudding.
    - Top with a layer of whipped cream.
- Repeat the layers until you reach the top of the trifle dish, finishing with a dollop of whipped cream on top.

6. Garnish:

- Garnish the trifle with fresh raspberries and chocolate shavings or curls.

7. Chill:

- Refrigerate the Chocolate Raspberry Brownie Trifle for at least 2-4 hours to allow the flavors to meld and the dessert to set.

8. Serve:

- Serve chilled and enjoy the layers of chocolatey, fruity goodness!

This Chocolate Raspberry Brownie Trifle is not only delicious but also a stunning dessert that's perfect for special occasions or gatherings. Feel free to customize it with additional layers or your favorite toppings!

Chocolate Pistachio Tart

Ingredients:

For the Crust:

- 1 1/2 cups chocolate cookie crumbs (you can use chocolate graham crackers or chocolate sandwich cookies)
- 1/3 cup unsalted butter, melted
- 1/4 cup granulated sugar

For the Chocolate Ganache Filling:

- 1 1/2 cups heavy cream
- 12 ounces dark chocolate, finely chopped
- 2 tablespoons unsalted butter, at room temperature

For the Pistachio Topping:

- 1 cup shelled pistachios, toasted and roughly chopped
- Pinch of salt (optional)
- Whipped cream or vanilla ice cream for serving (optional)

Instructions:

1. Prepare the Crust:

- Preheat your oven to 350°F (175°C).
- In a bowl, combine the chocolate cookie crumbs, melted butter, and granulated sugar. Mix until well combined.
- Press the mixture into the bottom and up the sides of a tart pan to form the crust.
- Bake the crust in the preheated oven for about 10 minutes. Allow it to cool completely.

2. Make the Chocolate Ganache Filling:

- In a saucepan, heat the heavy cream over medium heat until it just begins to simmer.

- Place the finely chopped dark chocolate in a heatproof bowl.
- Pour the hot cream over the chocolate, let it sit for a minute, and then stir until smooth.
- Add the room temperature butter and continue to stir until well combined and glossy.

3. Assemble the Tart:

- Pour the chocolate ganache into the cooled tart crust, spreading it evenly.
- Place the tart in the refrigerator to set for at least 2 hours or until the ganache is firm.

4. Add the Pistachio Topping:

- Once the ganache is set, remove the tart from the refrigerator.
- Sprinkle the toasted and roughly chopped pistachios over the chocolate ganache, pressing them gently into the surface.
- Optionally, add a pinch of salt over the pistachios for an extra flavor contrast.

5. Serve:

- Slice and serve the Chocolate Pistachio Tart at room temperature.
- Optionally, serve each slice with a dollop of whipped cream or a scoop of vanilla ice cream.

This Chocolate Pistachio Tart is a luxurious and decadent dessert with a perfect balance of textures and flavors. Enjoy it as a delightful treat for special occasions or any time you're craving something indulgent.

Mocha Chocolate Chip Cookies

Ingredients:

- 1 cup (2 sticks) unsalted butter, softened
- 1 cup granulated sugar
- 1 cup brown sugar, packed
- 2 large eggs
- 1 teaspoon vanilla extract
- 2 cups all-purpose flour
- 1/2 cup unsweetened cocoa powder
- 1 tablespoon instant coffee or espresso powder (adjust to taste)
- 1 teaspoon baking soda
- 1/2 teaspoon salt
- 2 cups chocolate chips (semisweet or dark)

Instructions:

1. Preheat Oven:

- Preheat your oven to 350°F (175°C). Line baking sheets with parchment paper.

2. Cream Butter and Sugars:

- In a large bowl, cream together the softened butter, granulated sugar, and brown sugar until light and fluffy.

3. Add Eggs and Vanilla:

- Add the eggs one at a time, beating well after each addition. Mix in the vanilla extract.

4. Combine Dry Ingredients:

- In a separate bowl, whisk together the flour, cocoa powder, instant coffee or espresso powder, baking soda, and salt.

5. Mix Wet and Dry Ingredients:

- Gradually add the dry ingredients to the wet ingredients, mixing until just combined.

6. Add Chocolate Chips:

    - Fold in the chocolate chips until evenly distributed throughout the cookie dough.

7. Drop Cookies:

    - Drop rounded tablespoons of dough onto the prepared baking sheets, leaving space between each cookie.

8. Bake:

    - Bake in the preheated oven for 10-12 minutes or until the edges are set. The centers may still look slightly undercooked, but they will continue to firm up as they cool.

9. Cool:

    - Allow the cookies to cool on the baking sheets for a few minutes before transferring them to a wire rack to cool completely.

10. Serve:

    - Once the Mocha Chocolate Chip Cookies are fully cooled, serve and enjoy with a glass of milk or a cup of coffee.

These cookies are perfect for coffee lovers and those who enjoy the combination of chocolate and a hint of coffee flavor. Enjoy the rich and decadent taste of Mocha Chocolate Chip Cookies!

Chocolate Strawberry Shortcake

Ingredients:

For the Chocolate Shortcakes:

- 2 cups all-purpose flour
- 1/2 cup cocoa powder
- 1/2 cup granulated sugar
- 1 tablespoon baking powder
- 1/2 teaspoon salt
- 1/2 cup unsalted butter, cold and cut into small pieces
- 1 cup milk
- 1 teaspoon vanilla extract

For the Chocolate Whipped Cream:

- 1 cup heavy cream
- 2 tablespoons cocoa powder
- 1/4 cup powdered sugar
- 1 teaspoon vanilla extract

For the Strawberry Filling:

- 1 pound fresh strawberries, hulled and sliced
- 2-3 tablespoons granulated sugar (adjust to taste)

Optional Garnish:

- Chocolate shavings or curls
- Fresh mint leaves

Instructions:

1. Prepare Chocolate Shortcakes:

- Preheat your oven to 425°F (220°C). Line a baking sheet with parchment paper.

- In a large bowl, whisk together the flour, cocoa powder, sugar, baking powder, and salt.
- Add the cold, cubed butter to the dry ingredients. Use a pastry cutter or your fingers to incorporate the butter until the mixture resembles coarse crumbs.
- Pour in the milk and vanilla extract. Stir until just combined.
- Turn the dough out onto a floured surface and gently knead it a few times. Pat the dough to about 1/2-inch thickness.
- Use a round biscuit cutter to cut out shortcakes and place them on the prepared baking sheet.
- Bake for 12-15 minutes or until the shortcakes are firm to the touch. Allow them to cool completely.

2. Prepare Chocolate Whipped Cream:

- In a chilled bowl, whip the heavy cream until soft peaks form.
- Add the cocoa powder, powdered sugar, and vanilla extract. Continue whipping until stiff peaks form.

3. Prepare Strawberry Filling:

- In a bowl, toss the sliced strawberries with granulated sugar. Let them sit for about 15-20 minutes to allow the strawberries to release their juices.

4. Assemble Chocolate Strawberry Shortcakes:

- Slice the chocolate shortcakes in half horizontally.
- Spoon a generous portion of the strawberry filling onto the bottom half of each shortcake.
- Top with a dollop of chocolate whipped cream.
- Place the other half of the shortcake on top.

5. Garnish:

- Garnish the Chocolate Strawberry Shortcakes with chocolate shavings or curls and fresh mint leaves if desired.

6. Serve:

- Serve the Chocolate Strawberry Shortcakes immediately and enjoy the delicious combination of chocolate, strawberries, and whipped cream.

This delightful dessert is perfect for celebrating special occasions or indulging in a sweet treat. The combination of chocolate, strawberries, and creamy whipped topping is sure to be a crowd-pleaser!

Peanut Butter Chocolate Fudge

Ingredients:

- 1 cup creamy peanut butter
- 1/2 cup unsalted butter
- 1 teaspoon vanilla extract
- 2 cups powdered sugar
- 1 1/2 cups semi-sweet chocolate chips
- A pinch of salt (optional)
- Chopped peanuts for garnish (optional)

Instructions:

1. Prepare the Pan:

- Line an 8x8-inch square baking pan with parchment paper, leaving some overhang for easy removal.

2. Melt Peanut Butter and Butter:

- In a medium-sized saucepan over medium heat, melt the peanut butter and unsalted butter together, stirring until smooth and well combined.

3. Add Vanilla Extract:

- Remove the saucepan from heat and stir in the vanilla extract. Mix well.

4. Add Powdered Sugar:

- Gradually add the powdered sugar to the peanut butter mixture, stirring until the mixture is smooth and free of lumps. It will form a thick, fudgy consistency.

5. Press into Pan:

- Press the peanut butter fudge mixture evenly into the prepared baking pan.

6. Melt Chocolate:

- In a microwave-safe bowl or using a double boiler, melt the chocolate chips until smooth. Stir in a pinch of salt if desired.

7. Spread Chocolate Layer:

- Pour the melted chocolate over the peanut butter layer in the pan, spreading it evenly with a spatula.

8. Swirl Layers:

- Use a knife or toothpick to create swirls or patterns by gently dragging it through the layers, creating a marbled effect.

9. Garnish (Optional):

- Sprinkle chopped peanuts on top of the fudge for an added crunch and visual appeal.

10. Chill:

- Place the pan in the refrigerator and let the Peanut Butter Chocolate Fudge set for at least 2-3 hours, or until it's firm.

11. Cut and Serve:

- Once the fudge is fully set, lift it out of the pan using the parchment paper overhang. Place it on a cutting board and cut it into squares.

12. Store:

- Store the fudge in an airtight container in the refrigerator. Bring it to room temperature before serving.

Enjoy the creamy and luscious combination of peanut butter and chocolate in this delightful fudge. It makes for a wonderful homemade gift or a sweet treat for any occasion!

Chocolate Mocha Cupcakes

Ingredients:

For the Cupcakes:

- 1 1/2 cups all-purpose flour
- 1/2 cup unsweetened cocoa powder
- 1 teaspoon baking powder
- 1/2 teaspoon baking soda
- 1/4 teaspoon salt
- 1 cup granulated sugar
- 1/2 cup unsalted butter, softened
- 2 large eggs
- 1 teaspoon vanilla extract
- 1 cup strong brewed coffee, cooled to room temperature

For the Mocha Buttercream Frosting:

- 1 cup unsalted butter, softened
- 3 cups powdered sugar
- 1/4 cup unsweetened cocoa powder
- 1-2 tablespoons instant coffee granules (adjust to taste)
- 2-3 tablespoons milk or cream
- 1 teaspoon vanilla extract

Instructions:

For the Cupcakes:

Preheat Oven:
- Preheat your oven to 350°F (175°C). Line a cupcake tin with paper liners.

Sift Dry Ingredients:
- In a bowl, sift together the flour, cocoa powder, baking powder, baking soda, and salt. Set aside.

Cream Butter and Sugar:
- In a large bowl, cream together the softened butter and sugar until light and fluffy.

Add Eggs and Vanilla:

- Add the eggs one at a time, beating well after each addition. Mix in the vanilla extract.

Combine Wet and Dry Ingredients:
- Gradually add the sifted dry ingredients to the wet ingredients, alternating with the brewed coffee. Begin and end with the dry ingredients. Mix until just combined.

Fill Cupcake Liners:
- Divide the batter evenly among the cupcake liners, filling each about two-thirds full.

Bake:
- Bake in the preheated oven for 18-20 minutes or until a toothpick inserted into the center of a cupcake comes out clean.

Cool:
- Allow the cupcakes to cool in the tin for a few minutes before transferring them to a wire rack to cool completely.

For the Mocha Buttercream Frosting:

Cream Butter:
- In a large bowl, beat the softened butter until creamy and smooth.

Add Cocoa and Coffee:
- Sift in the powdered sugar and cocoa powder. Add the instant coffee granules. Mix on low speed until combined.

Add Liquid and Vanilla:
- Add 2 tablespoons of milk or cream and the vanilla extract. Beat on medium-high speed until the frosting is smooth and fluffy. Add more milk if needed for the desired consistency.

Assembly:

Frost Cupcakes:
- Once the cupcakes are completely cooled, frost them with the Mocha Buttercream Frosting using a piping bag or a spatula.

Optional: Garnish:
- Garnish the cupcakes with chocolate shavings, a dusting of cocoa powder, or a coffee bean.

Serve:
- Serve and enjoy your delicious Chocolate Mocha Cupcakes!

These cupcakes are perfect for coffee and chocolate lovers alike. They make a great treat for special occasions or a delightful addition to any dessert spread.

Chocolate Cherry Cheesecake Bars

Ingredients:

For the Crust:

- 1 1/2 cups chocolate cookie crumbs (you can use chocolate graham crackers or chocolate sandwich cookies)
- 1/3 cup unsalted butter, melted
- 2 tablespoons granulated sugar

For the Cheesecake Filling:

- 16 ounces (2 packages) cream cheese, softened
- 1/2 cup granulated sugar
- 2 large eggs
- 1 teaspoon vanilla extract

For the Chocolate Ganache:

- 1 cup semisweet chocolate chips
- 1/2 cup heavy cream

For the Cherry Topping:

- 1 1/2 cups fresh or canned cherries, pitted and halved
- 2 tablespoons granulated sugar
- 1 tablespoon cornstarch
- 1 tablespoon water

Instructions:

1. Preheat Oven:

- Preheat your oven to 325°F (163°C). Line a 9x9-inch baking pan with parchment paper, leaving an overhang for easy removal.

2. Prepare the Crust:

- In a bowl, combine the chocolate cookie crumbs, melted butter, and granulated sugar. Press the mixture evenly into the bottom of the prepared baking pan to form the crust.

3. Bake the Crust:

    - Bake the crust in the preheated oven for about 10 minutes. Remove it from the oven and let it cool while you prepare the cheesecake filling.

4. Make the Cheesecake Filling:

    - In a large mixing bowl, beat the softened cream cheese and sugar until smooth and creamy.
    - Add the eggs one at a time, beating well after each addition. Mix in the vanilla extract until well combined.

5. Pour Over Crust:

    - Pour the cheesecake filling over the cooled crust, spreading it evenly.

6. Bake Cheesecake Layer:

    - Bake in the preheated oven for about 25-30 minutes or until the edges are set and the center is slightly jiggly.

7. Cool:

    - Allow the cheesecake layer to cool completely in the pan.

8. Make Chocolate Ganache:

    - In a heatproof bowl, combine the chocolate chips and heavy cream. Heat the mixture in the microwave or over a double boiler, stirring until smooth and well combined.

9. Pour Ganache Over Cheesecake:

- Pour the chocolate ganache over the cooled cheesecake layer, spreading it evenly.

10. Prepare Cherry Topping:

- In a saucepan, combine the cherries, sugar, cornstarch, and water. Cook over medium heat until the mixture thickens and the cherries are soft. Remove from heat and let it cool.

11. Add Cherry Topping:

- Spoon the cherry topping over the chocolate ganache layer.

12. Chill:

- Refrigerate the Chocolate Cherry Cheesecake Bars for at least 4 hours or overnight to allow them to set.

13. Slice and Serve:

- Once fully chilled, use the parchment paper overhang to lift the bars from the pan. Place them on a cutting board and slice into squares.

14. Optional: Garnish:

- Garnish the bars with additional chocolate shavings or a dusting of cocoa powder before serving.

Enjoy these decadent Chocolate Cherry Cheesecake Bars as a delightful treat for any occasion!

Chocolate Orange Scones

Ingredients:

For the Scones:

- 2 cups all-purpose flour
- 1/3 cup granulated sugar
- 1/4 cup unsweetened cocoa powder
- 1 tablespoon baking powder
- 1/2 teaspoon baking soda
- 1/2 teaspoon salt
- 1/2 cup cold unsalted butter, cut into small pieces
- 1/2 cup dark chocolate chips or chunks
- Zest of one orange
- 1/2 cup buttermilk
- 1 large egg
- 1 teaspoon vanilla extract

For the Orange Glaze:

- 1 cup powdered sugar
- 2-3 tablespoons fresh orange juice
- Zest of one orange

Instructions:

1. Preheat Oven:

- Preheat your oven to 400°F (200°C). Line a baking sheet with parchment paper.

2. Prepare Dry Ingredients:

- In a large bowl, whisk together the flour, sugar, cocoa powder, baking powder, baking soda, and salt.

3. Cut in Butter:

- Add the cold butter pieces to the dry ingredients. Use a pastry cutter or your fingers to cut the butter into the flour mixture until it resembles coarse crumbs.

4. Add Chocolate and Orange Zest:

- Stir in the dark chocolate chips or chunks and the orange zest.

5. Combine Wet Ingredients:

- In a separate bowl, whisk together the buttermilk, egg, and vanilla extract.

6. Mix Dough:

- Pour the wet ingredients into the dry ingredients and stir until just combined. Be careful not to overmix.

7. Form Dough:

- Turn the dough out onto a floured surface and gently knead it a few times. Pat the dough into a circle about 1-inch thick.

8. Cut Scones:

- Use a sharp knife or a round biscuit cutter to cut the dough into wedges or rounds.

9. Bake:

- Place the scones on the prepared baking sheet and bake in the preheated oven for 12-15 minutes or until the scones are set and a toothpick inserted into the center comes out clean.

10. Make Orange Glaze:

- While the scones are baking, prepare the orange glaze. In a bowl, whisk together the powdered sugar, fresh orange juice, and orange zest until smooth.

11. Glaze Scones:

- Once the scones are out of the oven and have cooled slightly, drizzle the orange glaze over the top.

12. Serve:

- Serve the Chocolate Orange Scones warm or at room temperature. Enjoy the delightful combination of chocolate and citrus flavors!

These scones make for a perfect breakfast treat or a delightful addition to your afternoon tea. The chocolate and orange pairing adds a touch of indulgence to this classic baked good.

Mexican Hot Chocolate

Ingredients:

- 4 cups milk (whole milk or a combination of whole and evaporated milk)
- 1 tablet (about 3 ounces) Mexican chocolate (such as Abuelita or Ibarra), chopped
- 2 tablespoons unsweetened cocoa powder
- 1/4 cup granulated sugar (adjust to taste)
- 1/4 teaspoon ground cinnamon
- Pinch of ground nutmeg (optional)
- Pinch of cayenne pepper (optional, for a spicy kick)
- 1/4 cup masa harina (corn flour) dissolved in 1/2 cup water
- Whipped cream, cinnamon sticks, or chocolate shavings for garnish (optional)

Instructions:

1. Prepare Ingredients:

- Chop the Mexican chocolate tablet into smaller pieces to help it melt easily.

2. Heat Milk and Chocolate:

- In a medium-sized saucepan, heat the milk over medium heat until it begins to simmer.
- Add the chopped Mexican chocolate, cocoa powder, sugar, ground cinnamon, nutmeg (if using), and cayenne pepper (if using). Stir continuously to ensure the chocolate dissolves and the mixture is well combined.

3. Add Masa Harina:

- In a separate bowl, dissolve masa harina in water, making sure there are no lumps. Gradually add this mixture to the simmering chocolate milk, stirring continuously.
- Continue to simmer and stir the mixture until it thickens slightly. This might take about 10-15 minutes.

4. Adjust Sweetness:

- Taste the hot chocolate and adjust the sweetness by adding more sugar if needed. Stir until the sugar is completely dissolved.

5. Serve:

- Once the Mexican Hot Chocolate has reached your desired consistency and sweetness, remove it from the heat.
- Ladle the hot chocolate into mugs and serve it warm.

6. Garnish (Optional):

- Garnish with a dollop of whipped cream, a cinnamon stick, or chocolate shavings if desired.

Mexican Hot Chocolate is perfect for warming up on chilly days or as a festive treat during holidays. The combination of chocolate, spices, and masa harina creates a unique and comforting flavor. Enjoy this delicious and traditional Mexican beverage!

Chocolate Caramel Pretzel Rods

Ingredients:

- 1 bag (about 10-12 ounces) pretzel rods
- 1 cup caramel candies (individually wrapped or caramel bits)
- 1 cup chocolate chips (semisweet or milk chocolate)
- 1 tablespoon vegetable oil or shortening
- Toppings (optional): chopped nuts, sprinkles, sea salt, crushed cookies, or colored sugar

Instructions:

1. Prep Pretzel Rods:

- Line a baking sheet with parchment paper or a silicone baking mat.
- Unwrap the caramel candies if they are individually wrapped.

2. Melt Caramel:

- In a microwave-safe bowl, melt the caramel candies according to the package instructions or heat them in 20-second intervals, stirring between each interval until smooth.

3. Dip Pretzels in Caramel:

- Dip each pretzel rod into the melted caramel, ensuring an even coating. Use a spoon or spatula to help spread the caramel evenly.
- Allow any excess caramel to drip off.

4. Place on Baking Sheet:

- Place the caramel-coated pretzel rods on the prepared baking sheet and let them set. You can place them in the refrigerator for a quicker setting process.

5. Melt Chocolate:

- In a microwave-safe bowl, melt the chocolate chips and vegetable oil or shortening in 20-second intervals, stirring between each interval until smooth.

6. Dip in Chocolate:

- Dip each caramel-coated pretzel rod into the melted chocolate, coating it completely. Allow any excess chocolate to drip off.

7. Add Toppings:

- While the chocolate is still wet, sprinkle your preferred toppings over the chocolate-coated pretzel rods. Options include chopped nuts, sprinkles, sea salt, crushed cookies, or colored sugar.

8. Let Set:

- Place the chocolate and caramel-coated pretzel rods back on the baking sheet to allow the chocolate to set. You can refrigerate them for faster setting.

9. Serve:

- Once the chocolate is fully set, your Chocolate Caramel Pretzel Rods are ready to be enjoyed.

These sweet and salty treats are perfect for parties, gatherings, or as a delightful homemade gift. The combination of caramel, chocolate, and pretzels creates a delicious contrast of flavors and textures. Enjoy!

Triple Chocolate Waffles

Ingredients:

- 2 cups all-purpose flour
- 1/2 cup cocoa powder
- 1/4 cup granulated sugar
- 1 tablespoon baking powder
- 1/2 teaspoon baking soda
- 1/4 teaspoon salt
- 2 large eggs
- 1 3/4 cups buttermilk
- 1/2 cup unsalted butter, melted
- 1 teaspoon vanilla extract
- 1 cup semisweet chocolate chips
- 1/2 cup white chocolate chips
- Whipped cream, chocolate sauce, and additional chocolate chips for topping (optional)

Instructions:

1. Preheat Waffle Iron:

- Preheat your waffle iron according to the manufacturer's instructions.

2. Mix Dry Ingredients:

- In a large bowl, whisk together the flour, cocoa powder, sugar, baking powder, baking soda, and salt.

3. Mix Wet Ingredients:

- In a separate bowl, beat the eggs and then add the buttermilk, melted butter, and vanilla extract. Mix well.

4. Combine Wet and Dry Ingredients:

- Pour the wet ingredients into the dry ingredients and stir until just combined. Be careful not to overmix; it's okay if there are a few lumps.

5. Add Chocolate Chips:

- Gently fold in the semisweet chocolate chips and white chocolate chips into the batter.

6. Cook Waffles:

- Lightly grease the waffle iron with cooking spray or a small amount of melted butter.
- Pour the batter onto the preheated waffle iron, spreading it evenly. Close the lid and cook according to the manufacturer's instructions until the waffles are golden brown and crisp.

7. Keep Warm:

- Place the cooked waffles on a baking sheet in a warm oven while you cook the remaining batter.

8. Serve:

- Serve the Triple Chocolate Waffles warm, topped with whipped cream, a drizzle of chocolate sauce, and additional chocolate chips if desired.

9. Enjoy:

- Enjoy these decadent waffles as a special breakfast treat or dessert!

These Triple Chocolate Waffles are a delightful way to indulge your chocolate cravings. The combination of cocoa powder, chocolate chips, and white chocolate creates a rich and satisfying flavor that chocolate lovers will appreciate.

Chocolate Raspberry Crepes

Ingredients:

For the Crepes:

- 1 cup all-purpose flour
- 2 tablespoons unsweetened cocoa powder
- 2 tablespoons granulated sugar
- 1/4 teaspoon salt
- 3 large eggs
- 1 1/4 cups milk
- 2 tablespoons melted butter
- 1 teaspoon vanilla extract

For the Filling:

- 1 cup fresh raspberries
- 1 cup chocolate chips or chunks (dark, semisweet, or milk chocolate)
- Whipped cream for topping
- Powdered sugar for dusting

Instructions:

1. Make the Crepe Batter:

- In a blender, combine the flour, cocoa powder, sugar, salt, eggs, milk, melted butter, and vanilla extract. Blend until smooth.

2. Rest the Batter:

- Allow the crepe batter to rest in the refrigerator for at least 30 minutes. This allows the flour to fully absorb the liquid and results in a smoother batter.

3. Cook the Crepes:

- Heat a non-stick skillet or crepe pan over medium heat. Lightly grease the pan with butter or cooking spray.

- Pour a small amount of crepe batter into the center of the pan, swirling it around to coat the bottom thinly.
- Cook the crepe for about 1-2 minutes until the edges begin to lift. Flip the crepe and cook the other side for an additional 1-2 minutes until cooked through.
- Repeat the process with the remaining batter, stacking the cooked crepes on a plate.

4. Assemble the Crepes:

- Lay each crepe flat and fill it with a handful of fresh raspberries and a sprinkle of chocolate chips or chunks.
- Fold or roll the crepe, enclosing the filling.

5. Serve:

- Arrange the filled crepes on a serving plate.
- Top the crepes with a dollop of whipped cream.
- Dust with powdered sugar just before serving.

6. Optional Garnish:

- Garnish with additional fresh raspberries and a drizzle of chocolate sauce if desired.

7. Enjoy:

- Serve immediately and enjoy these delightful Chocolate Raspberry Crepes!

These chocolate raspberry crepes are perfect for a romantic breakfast or a special dessert. The combination of the luscious chocolate and the tartness of fresh raspberries creates a wonderful flavor contrast that's sure to be a hit.

Mint Chocolate Chip Cheesecake

Ingredients:

For the Crust:

- 1 1/2 cups chocolate cookie crumbs
- 1/4 cup unsalted butter, melted
- 2 tablespoons granulated sugar

For the Cheesecake Filling:

- 4 packages (8 ounces each) cream cheese, softened
- 1 1/4 cups granulated sugar
- 4 large eggs
- 1 cup sour cream
- 1 teaspoon vanilla extract
- 1/2 teaspoon peppermint extract
- Green food coloring (optional)
- 1 cup mini chocolate chips

For the Mint Chocolate Ganache:

- 1/2 cup heavy cream
- 1 cup chocolate chips
- 1/2 teaspoon peppermint extract
- Green food coloring (optional)

Instructions:

1. Preheat Oven:

- Preheat your oven to 325°F (163°C). Grease a 9-inch springform pan.

2. Make the Crust:

- In a bowl, combine the chocolate cookie crumbs, melted butter, and granulated sugar. Press the mixture into the bottom of the prepared springform pan to form the crust. Use the back of a spoon to create an even layer.

3. Prepare the Cheesecake Filling:

- In a large mixing bowl, beat the cream cheese until smooth and creamy.
- Add the sugar and beat until well combined.
- Add the eggs one at a time, beating well after each addition.
- Mix in the sour cream, vanilla extract, peppermint extract, and green food coloring (if using), until the mixture is smooth and evenly colored.
- Gently fold in the mini chocolate chips.

4. Bake:

- Pour the cheesecake filling over the crust in the springform pan.
- Bake in the preheated oven for 55-65 minutes or until the edges are set, and the center is slightly jiggly.

5. Cool:

- Allow the cheesecake to cool in the oven with the door ajar for about an hour.
- Refrigerate the cheesecake for at least 4 hours or overnight to set.

6. Make the Mint Chocolate Ganache:

- In a saucepan, heat the heavy cream until it just begins to simmer.
- Remove from heat and add the chocolate chips. Let it sit for a minute, then stir until smooth.
- Stir in the peppermint extract and green food coloring (if using) until well combined.

7. Decorate:

- Pour the mint chocolate ganache over the chilled cheesecake, spreading it evenly.
- Optionally, garnish with additional mini chocolate chips or mint leaves.

8. Chill Again:

- Place the cheesecake back in the refrigerator to let the ganache set.

9. Serve:

- Once fully set and chilled, release the springform pan and transfer the Mint Chocolate Chip Cheesecake to a serving plate.
- Slice and serve chilled. Enjoy!

This Mint Chocolate Chip Cheesecake is a perfect dessert for mint chocolate lovers. Its creamy texture and refreshing flavor make it an ideal treat for special occasions or whenever you crave a delightful and indulgent dessert.

Chocolate Pomegranate Clusters

Ingredients:

- 1 cup dark chocolate chips or chopped dark chocolate
- 1 cup pomegranate seeds (from about 1 large pomegranate)
- 1/2 cup chopped nuts (such as almonds or pistachios)
- Sea salt for sprinkling (optional)

Instructions:

1. Prepare Pomegranate:

- Cut the pomegranate in half and gently tap the back of each half with a wooden spoon to release the seeds. Collect the seeds in a bowl.

2. Melt Chocolate:

- In a heatproof bowl, melt the dark chocolate chips or chopped chocolate using a double boiler or by microwaving in 20-second intervals, stirring between each interval until smooth.

3. Combine Ingredients:

- Add the pomegranate seeds and chopped nuts to the melted chocolate. Stir gently until all ingredients are evenly coated.

4. Form Clusters:

- Line a baking sheet with parchment paper or a silicone mat.
- Using a spoon, drop small clusters of the chocolate mixture onto the prepared baking sheet. You can make them as small or large as you prefer.

5. Set and Sprinkle:

- Allow the clusters to set at room temperature or place them in the refrigerator for quicker setting.

- If desired, sprinkle a pinch of sea salt over the clusters while the chocolate is still soft.

6. Serve:

- Once the clusters are fully set, transfer them to a serving plate.
- Serve and enjoy these Chocolate Pomegranate Clusters as a delightful and healthy treat!

These clusters make for a fantastic dessert or snack, combining the antioxidant-rich pomegranate seeds with the indulgence of dark chocolate. The addition of nuts provides a satisfying crunch. Enjoy the sweet and tart flavor combination!

Chocolate Hazelnut Brioche

Ingredients:

For the Brioche Dough:

- 2 1/4 teaspoons (1 packet) active dry yeast
- 1/4 cup warm water (about 110°F or 43°C)
- 1/2 cup granulated sugar
- 4 cups all-purpose flour
- 1 teaspoon salt
- 4 large eggs
- 1 cup unsalted butter, softened

For the Chocolate Hazelnut Filling:

- 1/2 cup chocolate hazelnut spread (such as Nutella)
- 1/2 cup finely chopped hazelnuts

For the Egg Wash:

- 1 egg
- 1 tablespoon milk or water

Optional:

- Powdered sugar for dusting

Instructions:

1. Activate Yeast:

- In a small bowl, combine the active dry yeast with warm water and a pinch of sugar. Let it sit for about 5-10 minutes until it becomes frothy.

2. Make Brioche Dough:

- In a large mixing bowl or the bowl of a stand mixer, combine the flour, sugar, and salt. Make a well in the center.
- Pour the activated yeast mixture into the well. Add the eggs one at a time, mixing well after each addition.
- Add the softened butter and knead the dough until it is smooth and elastic. This can be done by hand or with a stand mixer fitted with a dough hook attachment.
- Place the dough in a lightly greased bowl, cover it with a kitchen towel, and let it rise in a warm place for 1-2 hours or until doubled in size.

3. Preheat Oven:

- Preheat your oven to 375°F (190°C). Grease and flour a brioche pan or a standard loaf pan.

4. Roll Out Dough:

- On a floured surface, roll out the brioche dough into a rectangle, about 1/4 inch thick.

5. Spread Chocolate Hazelnut Filling:

- Spread the chocolate hazelnut spread evenly over the rolled-out dough, leaving a small border around the edges.
- Sprinkle the finely chopped hazelnuts over the chocolate hazelnut spread.

6. Roll and Shape:

- Starting from one of the long sides, tightly roll the dough into a log. Pinch the seam to seal.
- Place the rolled dough into the greased and floured brioche pan or loaf pan.

7. Let it Rise Again:

- Cover the pan with a kitchen towel and let the dough rise for another 30-45 minutes, or until it's puffy.

8. Brush with Egg Wash:

- In a small bowl, beat the egg with milk or water to create an egg wash. Brush the surface of the brioche with the egg wash.

9. Bake:

- Bake in the preheated oven for 25-30 minutes or until the brioche is golden brown and sounds hollow when tapped.

10. Cool and Dust:

- Allow the Chocolate Hazelnut Brioche to cool in the pan for 10 minutes before transferring it to a wire rack to cool completely.
- Once cooled, you can dust the top with powdered sugar if desired.

11. Slice and Serve:

- Slice the brioche and serve it as a delicious treat for breakfast, brunch, or dessert.

This Chocolate Hazelnut Brioche is a delightful twist on the classic brioche, and the combination of chocolate, hazelnuts, and buttery bread is sure to be a hit. Enjoy this indulgent treat with a cup of coffee or tea!

Chocolate Covered Espresso Beans

Ingredients:

- 1 cup whole espresso beans (dark roast recommended)
- 1 cup dark chocolate chips or chopped dark chocolate
- 1 tablespoon vegetable oil or coconut oil (optional, for thinning the chocolate)

Instructions:

1. Prepare Espresso Beans:

- Brew a strong cup of espresso or use pre-roasted espresso beans.

2. Melt Chocolate:

- In a heatproof bowl, melt the dark chocolate chips or chopped dark chocolate. You can do this using a double boiler or by microwaving in short 20-second intervals, stirring between each interval until smooth.
- If the chocolate is too thick, you can add vegetable oil or coconut oil to thin it out, making it easier to coat the espresso beans.

3. Coat Espresso Beans:

- Add the espresso beans to the melted chocolate, making sure they are fully coated.
- Using a fork or chocolate dipper, lift the chocolate-covered espresso beans, allowing excess chocolate to drip off.

4. Set on Parchment Paper:

- Place the coated espresso beans on a parchment paper-lined tray or baking sheet, making sure they are not touching each other.

5. Let Them Set:

- Allow the chocolate-covered espresso beans to set at room temperature or place them in the refrigerator for quicker setting.

6. Store:

- Once fully set, transfer the chocolate-covered espresso beans to an airtight container or a resealable bag.

7. Enjoy:

- Enjoy these homemade chocolate-covered espresso beans as a delightful snack or as a pick-me-up treat when you need a burst of energy!

Tip: You can experiment with different types of chocolate, such as milk or white chocolate, and even add a sprinkle of cocoa powder or a touch of sea salt for added flavor.

These chocolate-covered espresso beans make for a delicious treat, and they're perfect for coffee lovers who enjoy the combination of chocolate and the bold taste of espresso. They're also great as a homemade gift or a delightful addition to a coffee-themed gift basket.

White Chocolate Raspberry Blondies

Ingredients:

- 1 cup (2 sticks) unsalted butter, melted
- 2 cups light brown sugar, packed
- 2 large eggs
- 1 teaspoon vanilla extract
- 2 cups all-purpose flour
- 1/2 teaspoon baking powder
- 1/4 teaspoon baking soda
- 1/2 teaspoon salt
- 1 cup white chocolate chips or chunks
- 1 cup fresh or frozen raspberries

Instructions:

1. Preheat Oven:

- Preheat your oven to 350°F (175°C). Grease and flour a 9x13-inch baking pan or line it with parchment paper.

2. Melt Butter:

- In a microwave-safe bowl, melt the butter.

3. Mix Wet Ingredients:

- In a large mixing bowl, whisk together the melted butter and brown sugar until well combined.
- Add the eggs and vanilla extract, and mix until smooth.

4. Combine Dry Ingredients:

- In a separate bowl, whisk together the flour, baking powder, baking soda, and salt.

5. Mix Batter:

- Gradually add the dry ingredients to the wet ingredients, stirring until just combined. Be careful not to overmix.
- Fold in the white chocolate chips or chunks until evenly distributed in the batter.

6. Add Raspberries:

- Gently fold in the raspberries, being careful not to crush them too much.

7. Spread in Pan:

- Spread the blondie batter evenly into the prepared baking pan.

8. Bake:

- Bake in the preheated oven for 25-30 minutes or until the edges are golden brown and a toothpick inserted into the center comes out with a few moist crumbs.

9. Cool:

- Allow the blondies to cool completely in the pan on a wire rack.

10. Cut and Serve:

- Once cooled, cut the blondies into squares and serve.

11. Optional: Drizzle with White Chocolate:

- If desired, melt a bit of additional white chocolate and drizzle it over the top of the cooled blondies for an extra touch of sweetness.

12. Enjoy:

- Enjoy these White Chocolate Raspberry Blondies as a delicious dessert or snack!

These blondies are a perfect balance of sweet and tart flavors, making them a delightful treat for any occasion. The combination of white chocolate and raspberries creates a luscious and indulgent dessert that is sure to be a hit.

Dark Chocolate Sea Salt Caramels

Ingredients:

For the Caramel:

- 1 cup granulated sugar
- 1/2 cup unsalted butter
- 1/2 cup heavy cream
- 1/4 cup light corn syrup
- 1 teaspoon vanilla extract

For the Coating:

- 8 ounces dark chocolate (chopped or chocolate chips)
- Sea salt flakes for sprinkling

Instructions:

1. Prepare Baking Pan:

- Line an 8-inch square baking pan with parchment paper, leaving some overhang on the sides for easy removal later. Grease the parchment paper with butter or cooking spray.

2. Make Caramel:

- In a heavy-bottomed saucepan, combine sugar, butter, heavy cream, and corn syrup over medium heat. Stir continuously until the sugar dissolves and the mixture comes to a boil.
- Insert a candy thermometer into the mixture and continue cooking, without stirring, until it reaches 245°F (118°C) - this is the soft ball stage.
- Remove the saucepan from heat and stir in the vanilla extract.

3. Pour into Pan:

- Immediately pour the hot caramel into the prepared baking pan.

4. Let Caramels Set:

- Let the caramel cool and set for a few hours or overnight.

5. Cut into Squares:

- Once the caramel has fully set, use the parchment paper overhang to lift the block of caramel out of the pan. Place it on a cutting board.
- Using a sharp, buttered knife, cut the caramel into small squares.

6. Melt Dark Chocolate:

- In a microwave-safe bowl or using a double boiler, melt the dark chocolate until smooth.

7. Coat Caramels:

- Dip each caramel square into the melted dark chocolate, ensuring it is fully coated. Use a fork to lift the caramel out of the chocolate, allowing excess to drip off.

8. Place on Parchment:

- Place the chocolate-coated caramels on a parchment-lined tray or baking sheet.

9. Sprinkle with Sea Salt:

- While the chocolate is still wet, sprinkle each caramel with a pinch of sea salt flakes.

10. Let Chocolate Set:

- Allow the chocolate to set at room temperature or place the tray in the refrigerator for quicker setting.

11. Serve:

- Once the chocolate is fully set, transfer the Dark Chocolate Sea Salt Caramels to an airtight container or present them in decorative boxes.

12. Enjoy:

- Enjoy these delicious homemade treats as a sweet and salty indulgence!

These Dark Chocolate Sea Salt Caramels make for a wonderful gift or a decadent treat for special occasions. The combination of the smooth, rich caramel, dark chocolate, and the sprinkle of sea salt creates a delightful flavor profile that's sure to satisfy your sweet cravings.

Chocolate Banana Smoothie Bowl

Ingredients:

For the Smoothie:

- 2 ripe bananas, frozen
- 1/2 cup Greek yogurt
- 2 tablespoons cocoa powder
- 1 tablespoon almond butter or peanut butter
- 1/2 cup milk (dairy or plant-based)
- 1 teaspoon honey or maple syrup (optional, for added sweetness)
- Ice cubes (optional, for a thicker consistency)

For Toppings:

- Sliced bananas
- Chopped nuts (almonds, walnuts, or your choice)
- Granola
- Chia seeds
- Coconut flakes
- Dark chocolate shavings

Instructions:

1. Prepare Smoothie Base:

- In a blender, combine the frozen bananas, Greek yogurt, cocoa powder, almond butter, milk, and honey (if using). Blend until smooth.
- If you prefer a thicker consistency, you can add ice cubes and blend again until well combined.

2. Pour into a Bowl:

- Pour the chocolate banana smoothie into a bowl.

3. Add Toppings:

- Arrange your favorite toppings on top of the smoothie. Be creative and use a variety of textures and flavors.
- Sliced bananas, chopped nuts, granola, chia seeds, coconut flakes, and dark chocolate shavings work well as toppings.

4. Serve:

- Serve your Chocolate Banana Smoothie Bowl immediately and enjoy with a spoon.

5. Customize:

- Feel free to customize the smoothie bowl with additional fruits, seeds, or toppings of your choice.

6. Optional Drizzle:

- For an extra touch of sweetness, you can drizzle a bit of honey or maple syrup on top.

7. Enjoy:

- Enjoy your delicious and nutritious Chocolate Banana Smoothie Bowl!

This smoothie bowl is not only a treat for your taste buds but also a nutritious way to start your day. The combination of chocolate and banana provides a sweet and indulgent flavor, while the toppings add texture and additional health benefits.

Chocolate Pecan Cinnamon Rolls

Ingredients:

For the Dough:

- 1 cup warm milk (about 110°F or 43°C)
- 2 1/4 teaspoons active dry yeast (1 packet)
- 1/4 cup granulated sugar
- 1/4 cup unsalted butter, melted
- 1 teaspoon vanilla extract
- 1 large egg
- 4 cups all-purpose flour
- 1/2 teaspoon salt

For the Filling:

- 1/4 cup unsalted butter, softened
- 1/2 cup brown sugar, packed
- 2 tablespoons cocoa powder
- 1 tablespoon ground cinnamon
- 1 cup finely chopped pecans
- 1/2 cup chocolate chips or chunks

For the Frosting:

- 1/4 cup unsalted butter, softened
- 1 cup powdered sugar
- 2 tablespoons cream cheese, softened
- 1/2 teaspoon vanilla extract
- 1-2 tablespoons milk (adjust for desired consistency)

For Topping:

- Chopped pecans and chocolate shavings (optional)

Instructions:

1. Activate Yeast:

- In a bowl, combine warm milk, yeast, and a pinch of sugar. Let it sit for 5-10 minutes until frothy.

2. Make Dough:

    - In a large mixing bowl, combine the activated yeast mixture, melted butter, sugar, vanilla extract, and egg.
    - Gradually add the flour and salt, mixing until a dough forms.
    - Knead the dough on a floured surface for about 5-7 minutes until it becomes smooth and elastic.
    - Place the dough in a greased bowl, cover with a kitchen towel, and let it rise in a warm place for 1-2 hours or until doubled in size.

3. Prepare Filling:

    - In a bowl, mix together the softened butter, brown sugar, cocoa powder, ground cinnamon, chopped pecans, and chocolate chips.

4. Roll Out Dough:

    - Roll out the risen dough on a floured surface into a rectangle (about 12x18 inches).

5. Spread Filling:

    - Spread the filling mixture evenly over the rolled-out dough.

6. Roll and Cut:

    - Roll the dough tightly from the long edge to form a log. Cut the log into 12 equal slices.

7. Place in Pan:

    - Place the cinnamon rolls in a greased baking pan, leaving some space between each roll.

8. Let Them Rise Again:

- Cover the pan with a kitchen towel and let the rolls rise for an additional 30-45 minutes.

9. Preheat Oven:

- Preheat your oven to 375°F (190°C).

10. Bake:

- Bake the chocolate pecan cinnamon rolls in the preheated oven for 20-25 minutes or until golden brown.

11. Make Frosting:

- While the rolls are baking, prepare the frosting by mixing softened butter, powdered sugar, cream cheese, vanilla extract, and milk until smooth.

12. Frost and Top:

- Once the rolls are out of the oven, spread the frosting over them while they are still warm.
- Optionally, top with chopped pecans and chocolate shavings.

13. Serve:

- Serve the chocolate pecan cinnamon rolls warm and enjoy!

These Chocolate Pecan Cinnamon Rolls are a delightful combination of gooey chocolate, crunchy pecans, and soft cinnamon-infused dough. They make for a perfect treat for breakfast or brunch.

Chocolate Raspberry Soufflé

Ingredients:

- 1 cup fresh raspberries
- 2 tablespoons granulated sugar
- 1 tablespoon raspberry liqueur (optional)
- 1 cup semisweet or dark chocolate, chopped
- 1/2 cup unsalted butter
- 4 large eggs, separated
- 1/2 cup granulated sugar
- 1 teaspoon vanilla extract
- Pinch of salt
- Powdered sugar for dusting

Instructions:

1. Prepare Raspberries:

- In a small bowl, toss the fresh raspberries with 2 tablespoons of granulated sugar. Add raspberry liqueur if using. Set aside to macerate.

2. Preheat Oven:

- Preheat your oven to 375°F (190°C). Butter and sugar the ramekins or soufflé dishes.

3. Melt Chocolate and Butter:

- In a heatproof bowl set over a pot of simmering water (double boiler), melt the chopped chocolate and butter together. Stir until smooth. Remove from heat and let it cool slightly.

4. Add Egg Yolks:

- Whisk the egg yolks into the chocolate mixture one at a time. Add vanilla extract and continue to mix until well combined.

5. Whip Egg Whites:

    - In a clean, dry bowl, whip the egg whites with a pinch of salt until soft peaks form. Gradually add the granulated sugar and continue to whip until glossy and stiff peaks form.

6. Fold Egg Whites into Chocolate Mixture:

    - Gently fold one-third of the whipped egg whites into the chocolate mixture to lighten it.
    - Carefully fold in the remaining egg whites until no white streaks remain. Be gentle to keep the soufflé light and airy.

7. Fill Ramekins:

    - Spoon the chocolate mixture into the prepared ramekins, filling them almost to the top.

8. Add Raspberries:

    - Drop a few macerated raspberries into the center of each soufflé. The raspberries will sink a bit, and some will remain near the top.

9. Bake:

    - Place the filled ramekins on a baking sheet and bake in the preheated oven for about 15-18 minutes, or until the soufflés are puffed and set on top.

10. Dust with Powdered Sugar:

    - Remove the soufflés from the oven, dust with powdered sugar, and serve immediately.

11. Serve:

- Serve the Chocolate Raspberry Soufflés immediately, while they are still puffed and airy.

These Chocolate Raspberry Soufflés are a delightful way to end a special meal. The combination of rich chocolate and the burst of raspberry flavor creates a heavenly dessert that's sure to impress. Enjoy the magic of a perfectly risen soufflé!

Chocolate Almond Butter Cups

Ingredients:

For the Chocolate Coating:

- 1 cup semisweet or dark chocolate chips
- 2 tablespoons coconut oil

For the Almond Butter Filling:

- 1/2 cup almond butter (smooth or crunchy)
- 2 tablespoons powdered sugar
- 1/2 teaspoon vanilla extract
- A pinch of salt

Optional Toppings:

- Sea salt flakes
- Chopped almonds

Instructions:

1. Prepare a Muffin Tin:

   - Line a mini muffin tin with paper or silicone liners.

2. Melt Chocolate:

   - In a microwave-safe bowl or using a double boiler, melt the chocolate chips and coconut oil together until smooth. Stir well to combine.

3. Coat Muffin Cups:

   - Spoon a small amount of melted chocolate into the bottom of each lined muffin cup, spreading it up the sides a little.

4. Set Chocolate:

   - Place the muffin tin in the freezer for about 10-15 minutes or until the chocolate has set.

5. Prepare Almond Butter Filling:

   - In a bowl, mix together almond butter, powdered sugar, vanilla extract, and a pinch of salt until well combined.

6. Fill Cups:

   - Spoon a small amount of almond butter filling into each chocolate-coated cup, leaving some space around the edges.

7. Cover with Chocolate:

   - Pour the remaining melted chocolate over the almond butter filling in each cup, covering it completely.

8. Optional Toppings:

   - If desired, sprinkle sea salt flakes or chopped almonds on top of the chocolate before it sets.

9. Set in Freezer:

   - Place the muffin tin back in the freezer for about 20-30 minutes or until the chocolate is fully set.

10. Serve:

    - Once set, remove the chocolate almond butter cups from the muffin tin and peel away the liners.

11. Enjoy:

    - Enjoy these homemade Chocolate Almond Butter Cups as a delightful treat!

These chocolate almond butter cups are a fantastic alternative to store-bought peanut butter cups. They are customizable, and you can experiment with different nut butters, toppings, or even add a touch of sweetness to the filling according to your preference.

Black Forest Chocolate Cake

Ingredients:

For the Chocolate Cake:

- 2 cups all-purpose flour
- 2 cups granulated sugar
- 3/4 cup unsweetened cocoa powder
- 2 teaspoons baking powder
- 1 1/2 teaspoons baking soda
- 1 teaspoon salt
- 2 large eggs
- 1 cup whole milk
- 1/2 cup vegetable oil
- 2 teaspoons vanilla extract
- 1 cup boiling water

For the Cherry Filling:

- 2 cups fresh or canned cherries (pitted and halved)
- 1/2 cup granulated sugar
- 2 tablespoons cornstarch
- 1/4 cup water
- 1 tablespoon lemon juice
- 1/4 cup cherry liqueur or kirsch (optional)

For the Whipped Cream:

- 2 cups heavy whipping cream
- 1/4 cup powdered sugar
- 1 teaspoon vanilla extract

Optional Garnish:

- Chocolate shavings
- Maraschino cherries

Instructions:

1. Preheat Oven:

- Preheat your oven to 350°F (175°C). Grease and flour two 9-inch round cake pans.

2. Make Chocolate Cake:

- In a large bowl, sift together flour, sugar, cocoa powder, baking powder, baking soda, and salt.
- Add eggs, milk, oil, and vanilla extract. Mix until well combined.
- Stir in boiling water until the batter is smooth. The batter will be thin, but that's okay.
- Pour the batter evenly into the prepared cake pans.
- Bake in the preheated oven for 30-35 minutes or until a toothpick inserted into the center comes out clean.
- Allow the cakes to cool in the pans for 10 minutes, then transfer them to a wire rack to cool completely.

3. Make Cherry Filling:

- In a saucepan, combine cherries, sugar, cornstarch, water, and lemon juice.
- Cook over medium heat, stirring constantly until the mixture thickens and the cherries release their juices.
- Remove from heat and stir in cherry liqueur if using. Allow the filling to cool completely.

4. Make Whipped Cream:

- In a chilled bowl, whip the heavy whipping cream until soft peaks form.
- Add powdered sugar and vanilla extract, and continue whipping until stiff peaks form.

5. Assemble the Cake:

- Once the chocolate cake layers and cherry filling are completely cooled, place one cake layer on a serving plate.
- Spread a layer of whipped cream over the cake, followed by a layer of the cherry filling.
- Place the second cake layer on top and repeat the process, finishing with whipped cream on top.

6. Garnish:

- Garnish the cake with chocolate shavings and maraschino cherries if desired.

7. Refrigerate:

- Refrigerate the Black Forest Chocolate Cake for at least 2-3 hours or overnight before serving to allow the flavors to meld.

8. Serve:

- Slice and serve this delicious Black Forest Chocolate Cake. Enjoy!

This Black Forest Chocolate Cake is a showstopper dessert with layers of chocolatey goodness, tart cherries, and airy whipped cream. It's perfect for special occasions or whenever you want to treat yourself to a delightful and classic dessert.

Chocolate Covered Macadamia Nuts

Ingredients:

- 1 cup macadamia nuts
- 1 cup semisweet or dark chocolate chips
- 1 tablespoon coconut oil or vegetable shortening (optional, for smoothness)

Instructions:

1. Prep the Macadamia Nuts:

- Make sure the macadamia nuts are clean and dry. You can toast them lightly in a pan over medium heat for a few minutes to enhance their flavor, but this step is optional.

2. Melt the Chocolate:

- In a microwave-safe bowl or using a double boiler, melt the chocolate chips. If using the microwave, heat the chocolate in 20-second intervals, stirring between each interval until smooth. If desired, add coconut oil or vegetable shortening to the melted chocolate to achieve a smoother consistency.

3. Coat the Nuts:

- Add the macadamia nuts to the melted chocolate, making sure they are fully coated. Use a fork or chocolate dipper to lift the nuts, allowing excess chocolate to drip off.

4. Set on Parchment Paper:

- Place the chocolate-covered macadamia nuts on a parchment paper-lined tray or baking sheet, ensuring they are not touching each other.

5. Let Them Set:

- Allow the chocolate-covered macadamia nuts to set at room temperature or place them in the refrigerator for quicker setting.

6. Optional: Drizzle or Additional Toppings:

- If desired, you can drizzle some extra melted chocolate over the top of the set nuts for added decoration. Additionally, sprinkle a pinch of sea salt or coconut flakes while the chocolate is still soft.

7. Store:

- Once fully set and hardened, transfer the chocolate-covered macadamia nuts to an airtight container.

8. Enjoy:

- Enjoy these homemade chocolate-covered macadamia nuts as a delightful snack or gift!

These chocolate-covered macadamia nuts make for a wonderful treat, combining the creamy texture of macadamia nuts with the sweetness of chocolate. They are perfect for snacking, parties, or as a thoughtful homemade gift.

Chocolate Raspberry Chia Pudding

Ingredients:

- 1/4 cup chia seeds
- 1 cup milk (dairy or plant-based)
- 2 tablespoons cocoa powder
- 2-3 tablespoons maple syrup or honey (adjust to taste)
- 1/2 teaspoon vanilla extract
- A pinch of salt
- Fresh raspberries for topping
- Dark chocolate shavings for garnish (optional)

Instructions:

1. Prepare the Chia Pudding Base:

- In a bowl or jar, combine chia seeds, milk, cocoa powder, maple syrup (or honey), vanilla extract, and a pinch of salt.

2. Mix Well:

- Whisk the ingredients together thoroughly to ensure the chia seeds are well distributed and don't clump together.

3. Let It Set:

- Cover the bowl or jar and refrigerate the mixture for at least 4 hours or preferably overnight. This allows the chia seeds to absorb the liquid and create a pudding-like consistency.

4. Stir Again:

- After the initial setting time, give the chia pudding a good stir to break up any clumps and ensure a smooth texture.

5. Assemble the Chocolate Raspberry Chia Pudding:

- Spoon a layer of the chocolate chia pudding into serving glasses or bowls.
- Add a layer of fresh raspberries on top of the chocolate chia pudding.
- Repeat the layers until the glasses are filled, ending with a layer of raspberries on top.

6. Garnish:

- Optionally, garnish with dark chocolate shavings for added richness.

7. Serve:

- Serve the Chocolate Raspberry Chia Pudding chilled.

8. Enjoy:

- Enjoy this delightful and nutrient-packed chocolate raspberry treat!

This Chocolate Raspberry Chia Pudding is not only delicious but also packed with fiber, omega-3 fatty acids, and antioxidants from the chia seeds and raspberries. It makes for a satisfying and guilt-free dessert or a wholesome breakfast option. Feel free to customize the sweetness and toppings according to your taste preferences.